THE PSYCHO-LOGICAL WAY/ THE SPIRITUAL WAY

THE PSYCHO-LOGICAL WAY/ THE SPIRITUAL WAY

Martin & Deidre Bobgan

BETHANY HOUSE PUBLISHERS
MINNEAPOLIS, MINNESOTA 55438
A Division of Bethany Fellowship, Inc.

Passages excerpted from *The Myth of Psychotherapy* by Thomas Szasz. Copyright © 1978 by Thomas Szasz. Reprinted by permission of Doubleday and Company, Inc.

Published by Bethany Fellowship, Inc.
6820 Auto Club Road, Minneapolis, Minnesota 55438

Printed in the United States of America

Library of Congress Cataloging in Publication Data

Bobgan, Martin, 1930-
   The psychological way/the spiritual way.

   Bibliography: p.
   1. Pastoral counseling. 2. Pastoral psychology.
   3. Psychotherapy. I. Bobgan, Deidre, 1935-   joint author.
   II. Title.
   BV4012.2.B56   253.5   79-17884
   ISBN 0-87123-026-7

Lovingly dedicated
to our children,
Greg, Margot,
Raymond, and Janet

Martin Bobgan is Administrative Dean of the Continuing Education Division of Santa Barbara City College. He received a B.A., a B.S., and an M.A. in Educational Administration from the University of Minnesota, and an Ed.D in Educational Psychology from the University of Colorado. Before holding his present position, Martin was a college and university extension and summer session instructor in Educational Psychology. ***Deidre Bobgan*** received a B.S. degree in English from the University of Minnesota and an M.A. from the University of California. The Bobgans are co-directors of Counseling Ministry, Living Faith Center, Santa Barbara, California.

Acknowledgments

We are especially grateful to Rev. Herman Grams for his encouragement and confidence as we taught the principles presented in this book and developed a spiritual counseling ministry in our church. We would particularly like to thank Dr. Kent Norman, Associate Professor of Psychology at the University of Maryland, for his prayerful and extensive critiquing of an early draft of the book. Our many thanks also go to Mrs. Evalyn Stafford for reviewing the manuscript.

Authors' Note

Although it is desirable to read this book from beginning to
end in the normal fashion, it is not necessary to do so. Some
readers may wish to skip the research presented in Parts One
through Three and begin at Part Four to read about the various psychotherapeutic approaches. Others may wish to begin
at Part Six to read about the contrast and comparison between the psychological way and the spiritual way. While the
sequence in the book is a logical one, any one of the parts can
be read by itself.

Preface

There is a psychological way and a spiritual way to mental-emotional health. The psychological way is the way of psychotherapy, which is simply the treatment of mental-emotional disorders by psychological, man-made means. Through the application of techniques based on psychological theories, a psychotherapist attempts to assist a person to change attitudes, feelings, perceptions, values, and behavior. Psychotherapists are individuals who are trained and licensed to perform a wide variety of therapies. They include such persons as psychiatrists, psychoanalysts, clinical psychologists, marriage and family counselors, and some social workers. In addition, many individuals practice psychotherapy without a license and many of the new self-help systems are psychotherapies in practice without being named as such.

The true spiritual way, on the other hand, is based on the Bible. Rather than using theories of men, the spiritual counselor relies on the truths of God. Through such scriptural means as love, listening, acceptance, mercy, teaching, and encouragement, the spiritual counselor guides an individual in applying biblical principles to his life in order to develop more Christlike thought and behavior patterns.

Although the spiritual way has existed for thousands of years, the psychological way is relatively new. During the past eighty years, as people began to trust the psychological way more than the spiritual way, psychotherapy displaced the ministry of spiritual counseling. Today people wholeheartedly believe that psychotherapy, dressed in a wide variety of styles and shades, contains the secrets and answers for the healing of troubled souls. Many are confident of the curative power of psychotherapy in spite of the lack of substantial proof of its effectiveness. They believe many things about psychotherapy which are either untrue or have never been proven. Persuaded by the claims of psychotherapists, these individuals do not disbelieve or even question the validity of such claims.

Most people do not realize that psychotherapy is a belief system similar to that of a religion. Psychotherapeutic beliefs and religious beliefs both rest upon a foundation of faith. Many aspects of the psychotherapeutic faith systems will be examined in this book and the following questions considered: Does psychotherapy really work? Is psychotherapy based on observable, verifiable fact or on subjective theories and inter-pretations? To what extent is psychotherapy medicine, phil-osophy, or religion? On what ideologies are the various psy-chotherapeutic systems founded? Are Christianity and psy-chotherapy truly compatible? Finally, the question of Chris-tians as counselors will be examined and a challenge given to the church to restore the original practice of ministering to troubled souls.

Most Christians agree that the Scriptures are a basis for mental-emotional health, but very few seem to believe that the Bible is sufficient to deal with all nonorganically caused mental-emotional disorders. Many in the church believe that the Bible provides preventative principles for mental-emotional well-being but hesitate to accept that the Bible contains restorative power. We maintain that God and His Word provide a completely sufficient foundation for mental-emotional health and that the Bible is the repository of the healing balm for all nonorganically based mental-emotional disorders. To support this position, much of the book is devot-ed to exposing the weaknesses of psychotherapy in contrast to spiritual counseling which is based on biblical principles and power. We are not opposed to, nor are we criticizing, the entire field of psychology, but rather the practice of psychotherapy based on ideologies which contradict Scripture.

We believe that all nonorganically related mental-emotional disorders have a spiritual, Christ-centered solution rather than a psychological, self-centered solution. However, because psychotherapy has become such an integral part of our culture, this position may evoke an extreme reaction from many, including those Christians who through training or current professional involvement have vested interests and commitments in the field of psychotherapy. Nevertheless, this book is intended to provide a spiritual alternative in the area of mental-emotional healing and an encouragement for the restoration of the spiritual remedy for healing those people who suffer from mental-emotional disorders.

Table of Contents

1. The Popularity of Psychotherapy

Psychotherapy (the psychological way) is big business in America. As a nation we spend about 17 billion dollars every year for mental health.[1] While it is difficult to give an exact figure, almost ten percent, or about twenty million people, have either been in or are now in some sort of therapy. A recent report from the President's Commission on Mental Health indicates that the psychological profession now believes that twenty-five percent of the population needs professional help.[2] In fact the demand for therapy is so great that it has by far exceeded the number of available trained psychotherapists.[3]

The popularity of psychology and psychotherapy continues to soar. Perry London in his article "The Psychotherapy Boom" points out that psychology is the most popular major among American college students. He further reports:

> No branch of psychology, however, has grown so rapidly, done so well commercially or shown so little sign of slowdown as psychotherapy. If psychologists in general have been fruitful and multiplied, psychotherapists in particular have been fecund beyond measure.[4]

With respect to the future he predicts, " . . . the entire therapy business will continue to expand, barring economic disaster or political repression, to become a major service industry in a society dominated by service industries." [5]

Modern psychotherapy is less than eighty years old, but during this period of time it has influenced and changed modern man's way of thinking about himself and about the very meaning of life. He has been trained over these years to have great confidence in psychotherapy for the healing of mental-emotional problems. Not only does he have confidence in it, he has been conditioned to believe that if he doubts, questions, or contradicts psychotherapy, there must be something wrong with him. He has been led to believe that only non-thinking, naive individuals have such thoughts and that the intelligent and informed accept psychotherapy as the healing "balm of Gilead."

In the beginning, both the theory and the practice of psychotherapy were questioned and even ridiculed by medical doctors, ministers, and many others. But now this craze has so taken hold of veritably every walk of life that to doubt or disagree is to be narrow-minded, nonintelligent, or maybe even neurotic. After all, who are we to criticize or contradict something so seemingly useful as psychotherapy?

From the beginning of psychotherapy at the turn of the century, psychotherapeutic definitions of mental-emotional disorders have progressively expanded to include a vast array of mild maladies. Thus, the number of people considered to be in need of help has dramatically increased. Ralph Nader's Study Group Report on the National Institute of Mental Health expresses the view that "the great majority of those individuals labeled 'mentally ill' are in no way sick." [6] The authors of *The Madness Establishment* contend, "It is clear that out of the tens of millions of individuals whom NIMH officials and others estimate need psychiatric care, only a tiny minority suffer from problems that most authorities would agree constitute 'mental diseases.' " [7]

Nevertheless, psychotherapy is frantically being sought by a sensitive (and mostly not sick) society seeking a psychological solution for an internal anxiety that often has no real external justification. Myriads of people are going to therapists for a wide variety of discomforts that merely represent one form of anxiety or another. Some people even go because they suspect that there must be more to life than what they are experiencing. Jerome Frank declares:

> . . . too many people today have too much money and not enough to do, and they turn to psychotherapy to combat the resulting boredom. It supplies novelty, excitement and, as a means of self-improvement, a legitimate way of spending money. Today hosts of persons seek psychotherapy for discomforts that a less affluent society would regard as trivial.[8]

Psychotherapists, in turn, are eager to deal with these discomforts. According to the Ralph Nader research group, "A distressingly large number of mental health professionals take the position that everyone who walks into their offices needs therapy, frequently long-term therapy, which often stretches for several years to the tune of thousands of dollars." [9]

Frank notes: "Our psychotherapeutic literature has contained precious little on the redemptive power of suffering, acceptance of one's lot in life, filial piety, adherance to tradition, self-restraint and moderation." [10] Leo Rosten believes the title of his article, that "Unhappiness Is Not a Disease." He says:

> As recently as 30 years ago, no one questioned your right to be unhappy. Happiness was considered a blessing, not a guarantee. You were permitted to suffer pain, or fall into moods, or seek solitude without being analyzed, interpreted and discussed.[11]

Many people look to psychotherapy to make them happy, to escape the pain of living, and to find fulfillment and satisfaction. As long as they look to psychotherapy with hope and expectancy, the popularity of psychotherapy will continue to soar.

2. Does Psychotherapy Help?

Psychotherapy is popular and expensive, but is it generally helpful? Psychotherapists, patients, parents, pastors, and the public apparently think so. But is it really? Until about 1950, the general assumption was that psychotherapy did indeed work and was, of course, useful. The answer was demonstrated by testimonies of both psychotherapists and patients. Psychotherapists produced thousands of books, and patients testified to recovery, readjustment, and rejuvenation. Patients recovered from insecurity and insomnia, they readjusted to family situations, and they were rescued from despair and depression. The media reinforced these testimonials by romanticizing the psychotherapist and by regarding him as the "saviour" of troubled souls.[12]

The truth is that as long as we depend upon subjective statements of individuals rather than collected research, we can prove just about anything we want. And what was "proven" until about 1950 by virtue of personal testimonies was that psychotherapy was a gloriously successful method for treating the maladies and malaise of human maladjustment.

In the fifties more research began to be performed and in 1952 Hans J. Eysenck, an eminent English scholar, published a monograph in which he evaluated the effectiveness of psychotherapy. Although this treatise has been considered an insult by many, it was regarded as an inspiration by others. The technique Eysenck used has become a basis for numerous research studies since the publication of his article.

Eysenck compared groups of patients treated by psychotherapy with persons given little or no treatment at all. He listed twenty-four different reports of the results of psychotherapy, which included a total of 8,053 cases. Of these, 760 were treated by psychoanalysis and 7,293 by eclectic psychotherapy, which is any combination of a variety of psychotherapeutic techniques.

Eysenck found the improvement rate to be 44 percent for those receiving psychoanalysis, 64 percent for those treated by a variety of psychotherapeutic techniques, and 72 percent for those who did not receive any specific therapy at all.[13] In other words, a greater percentage of patients who did not have psychotherapy improved over those who did undergo therapy. One is not only impressed with the number of patients involved, but astounded at the results!

From his research, Eysenck concluded that "roughly two-thirds of a group of neurotic patients will recover or improve to a marked extent within about two years of the onset of their illness, whether they are treated by means of psychotherapy or not." Since his study failed to prove the advantage of psychotherapy over no treatment, he remarked, "From the point of view of the neurotic, these figures are encouraging; from the point of view of the psychotherapist, they can hardly be called very favorable to his claims." [14]

We are not trying to convince the reader that psychotherapy does not work at all. We are merely showing a transition period from the use of testimonials to the use of research as a basis for determining the effectiveness of psychotherapy. Additionally, we use this one monograph as an example of the research that followed and continues today, which lays bare the possible weaknesses of the once naively glorified practice of psychotherapy.

The conclusions of Eysenck's study stunned and embarrassed the psychotherapeutic world. The psychotherapists had been so deluded by testimonies and so confident of their techniques and apparent successes that they became infuriated with Eysenck and refused to believe the results of his research. Written rebuttals and reactions soon followed, but the monograph had made its mark and the door of doubt had been knocked ajar. The once glorious image of psychotherapy had been tarnished by a simple technique of comparison. The entire field had begun to be dissected by a device of research which may eventually divulge enough information to lead to its complete devaluation.

Although at that time few of the media publicized it and few people outside the field of psychology read the research, Pandora's box had been opened. This one monograph by Eysenck began a small but definite movement toward a careful analysis of the ritual and romance of psychotherapy.

Fifteen years later in 1967 Eysenck reported:

> To date, then, there is no real evidence for the effectiveness of psychotherapy—as is now admitted even by leading psychoanalysts and psychotherapists—though with further search such evidence might be uncovered.[15]

Two other researchers, Truax and Carkhuff, agree:

> . . . after a careful review of the relevant research literature, it now appears that Eysenck was essentially correct in saying that *average* counseling and psychotherapy as it is currently practiced does not result in average client improvement

greater than that observed in clients who receive no special counseling or psychotherapeutic treatment.[16]

Numerous studies since Eysenck's have used his method of comparing treated and untreated patients. In addition, various other methods and techniques have been employed to evaluate psychotherapy. One can now list a large number of studies on both sides of this issue. Some studies show that the unanalyzed, untreated, uncounseled, and untherapized patients get better at the same rate or at a greater rate than those treated, counseled and therapized. Other studies indicate that psychotherapy does make a difference and that treated patients do have a higher recovery rate than those not treated.

In "Comparative Studies of Psychotherapies" the authors examined thirty-three well-controlled studies comparing psychotherapeutically treated with nontherapeutically treated persons. Twenty of these studies favored psychotherapy, but thirteen indicated no significant difference in improvement between the treated and untreated groups of individuals.[17] Every one of the researchers agrees that patients get well both with and without psychotherapy. One researcher even believes that "All mental disorders . . . are not continuous . . . most, if not all, eventually disappear even without therapeutic intervention." [18]

The questions then remain. Do more patients get well with therapy or without any therapeutic treatment? If one's chances of getting better favor therapy, how much greater is the chance of success? In their attempt to understand the effectiveness of psychotherapy, researchers recognize the magnitude of these questions and the difficulty of adequately determining the value and the results of various forms of psychotherapeutic treatment.

In the book *Psychotherapy for Better or Worse*, the authors conclude that "the urgent question being pressed by the public—Does psychotherapy work?—goes unanswered." [19] One of the authors, Suzanne Hadley, elsewhere declares:

. . . the question itself, "Does psychotherapy work?" is at best a simplistic approach which defies an answer. Clinicians have failed to agree among themselves on what it means for psychotherapy to "work"—or to fail; nor is there agreement concerning what is and is not psychotherapy.[20]

Such statements indicate that we have been too naive from the very beginning and need to take a more objective stance.

It is not our purpose to review a large number of studies either for or against the efficacy of psychotherapy. Rather, the important point is that, whereas at one time in the history of psychotherapy people depended upon "word of mouth" to support an assumption that psychotherapy was an enormously successful endeavor, many now recognize that it was only an assumption based upon ignorance and enthusiasm, subjective opinion and hearsay.

We are not attempting to prove that psychotherapy does or does not work. We are only stressing that the research justifies a shift in our thinking, from one of unquestioning confidence in psychotherapy to one of reasonable doubt. Anyone who still believes in the romantic idea of the marvelous healing power of psychotherapy is out of touch with the stark reality of recent research.

3. Could Psychotherapy Be Harmful?

Related to the question of positive results of psychotherapy is the problem of possible negative effects. Some people view psychotherapy somewhat the same as they view the use of vitamin supplements: while at their best vitamins may be helpful, at their worst they are harmless. This seems to be the prevailing view of psychotherapy: it can be helpful, but at least it can't hurt anyone. According to recent research, such a view is false.

In medical literature there is a word used for unexpected detrimental effects of taking medicine or receiving other medical treatment. This word is *iatrogenic*. For example, a person may come to a medical doctor with a cold, receive antibiotics, and then suffer negative reactions to the antibiotics. This negative effect is called an *iatrogenic effect*. It is an adverse, though unexpected, result of treatment.

A similar effect is seen in various research studies in the field of psychotherapy. While improvement may occur under treatment, a patient may also get worse or deteriorate as a result of the therapy. Psychotherapy may be helpful to a person, but it may also be harmful. A book by Richard B. Stuart entitled *Trick or Treatment, How and When Psychotherapy Fails* is filled with studies and reviews that show "how current psychotherapeutic practices often harm the patients they are supposed to help." [21] In his conclusion, Stuart says:

> The extensive research reviewed in this book has shown that, compared with patients who receive no treatment or very limited treatment, those who receive both in- and out-patient treatment have a small chance of experiencing marked improvement, a very great chance of experiencing little or no change and a small chance of experiencing deterioration.[22]

One group of researchers surveyed 150 "expert clinicians, theoreticians, and researchers" on the negative effects of psychotherapy. They received seventy responses, which they say "represent a spectrum of contemporary thinking of some of the best minds in the field of psychotherapy." [23] The researchers conclude:

> It is clear that negative effects of psychotherapy are overwhelmingly regarded by experts in the field as a significant problem requiring the attention and concern of practitioners and researchers alike.[24]

We are not attempting to dramatize the iatrogenic effects of psychotherapy by quoting the various percentage figures from the numerous studies. They range from insignificantly small to astronomically large.[25] The average figure in the literature appears to be approximately ten percent, but even that has been questioned. Important here is the idea that most people never suspected such an effect from psychotherapy until researchers brought the possibility to our attention. After all, how could talking and listening hurt anyone?

Although there is disagreement as to the amount of harm that may occur in psychotherapy, there is no question that deterioration can and does occur. We do not fully understand why and how, but we know that negative effects do result from therapy. Because of this possibility, someone once suggested that every therapist should be required to have a sign over his door that reads: "Psychotherapy may be harmful to your mental health."

4. The Psychotherapeutic Marketplace

In the psychotherapeutic marketplace there are about 200 different therapeutic approaches and over 10,000 specific techniques available to the consumer.[26] Morris Parloff reports:

> New schools emerge constantly, heralded by claims that they provide better treatment, amelioration, or management of the problems and neuroses of the day. No school has ever withdrawn from the field for failure to live up to its claims, and as a consequence all continue to co-exist.[27]

All continue to exist and all claim success in spite of the fact that the various techniques, as well as the theories on which they rest, often contradict each other. For instance, one therapeutic technique may encourage freedom from responsibility while another may place a high value on personal responsibility. One is now led to the conclusion that any kind of therapy may work, no matter how silly or satanic it may be. However, as we have seen, people also improve without any therapy at all.

The number of therapies is proliferating greatly, so much so that it would be difficult to imagine a form of psychotherapy that has not already been conceived and practiced. Such forms of psychotherapy range all the way from very simple ones which may include lying to the patient by telling him that he is getting better (even when the therapist knows he is not getting better) to physically active ones which require the patient to vomit whether he wants to or not.

We have facetiously suggested that we could contrive a theory and give it either a simple title, such as "Theory X," or some esoteric title that no one understands, such as "Osmotic Therapy." To make it saleable, we could select several available concepts from any psychology text. Then to make it particularly appealing, we could add some trinitarian structure similar to Freud's id, ego, and superego; or Harris' Parent,

Adult, and Child; or Sullivan's good-me, bad-me, and not-me; or Glasser's reality, responsibility, and right-and-wrong.

Next we would need to write a simple book about it that could be easily understood by the general public, set up an institute (preferably in Los Angeles or New York) and hire a staff. Then, after the initial success, we would contact the media and tell the world about our unrivaled triumphs, ignore or conceal our failures, and promise unsurpassed miracles of happiness, adjustment, solutions to personal problems, and even physical healing. Finally, we would have to make room for the lonely, bored, frustrated, and anxiety-ridden masses who would flock to our door.

We are not accusing all psychotherapists of being dishonest or merely fabricating therapies out of whole cloth. We are only pointing out how gullible and desperate people are. They have been so indoctrinated about the need to flock to some psychological healer for relief from anxiety and guilt that they rush in without any understanding of the limitations or potential harm.

Many call psychotherapy a cure; others consider it a curse. At its worst it is considered a distortion and a deceit based solely upon the testimonies and hopes of therapists and their clients. At its best it is claimed to be a universal balm for all mankind. However, because the results of psychotherapy are both questionable and unpredictable, the most objective view might be this: psychotherapy helps some people at the risk of harming others.

Considering the evidence of the research studies, which indicate the questionability of success and the possibility of failure and negative effects, it is amazing that the majority of society places such enormous confidence in a system supported by a sparcity of proof and pays such high prices in hopes of the promised land. We must all accept some of the blame for this massive deception. The media has uncritically presented psychotherapy through rose-colored glasses and we have accepted it as the "holy grail of health."

While many are well-meaning, the psychotherapists are the ones who must accept the greatest blame and responsibility. How could they have so glibly pandered their wares in the human marketplace with so much zeal and confidence, without critically examining the results and cautioning the consumer of the danger of deterioration as well as the suspicions of success? The consumer needs to be warned of the potential danger and of the limited possibility of cure.

Since the rise of psychotherapy we have never before had such harsh criticisms of it, nor such suspicions of its supposed success, nor alarms at the degree of its dangers. Thomas Szasz in his recent book *The Myth of Psychotherapy* declares:

> My point is rather that many, perhaps most, so-called psychotherapeutic procedures are harmful for the so-called patients . . . and that all such interventions and proposals should therefore be regarded as evil until they are proven otherwise.[28]

Furthermore, Michael Scriven, a member of the American Psychological Association Board of Social and Ethical Responsibility, questions "the moral justification for dispensing psychotherapy, given the state of outcome studies which would lead the FDA to ban its sale if it were a drug." [29]

5. Christians and Psychotherapy

In view of all this contradictory evidence, why do people, and especially Christians, exhibit such confidence in psychotherapy? Why is it that when Christians experience problems in their lives they turn to this craze? Why do Christian schools and colleges offer these theories as facts? Why do priests and ministers so readily refer their people with problems to licensed professional psychotherapists?

We would like to suggest that the Christians were probably naturally suspicious of it at the beginning. However, now that they have uncritically accepted it, they seem reluctant to assume even a reasonably skeptical view. Could it be that, in an attempt to overcome their former image of narrow-mindedness, they have become naive? Or is it because they fear to challenge a system which they do not fully understand? Or is it because principles of psychotherapy and psychology have sometimes been so carefully interwoven with biblical principles that the Christian cannot separate the two? Maybe the sheer volume of people with problems has driven the ministers and all of us to refer problem-laden people away.

However, the main reason why Christians have placed such inordinate confidence in psychotherapy may be that they have lost their confidence in spiritual solutions for mental-emotional disorders. In a book entitled *The Crisis in Psychiatry and Religion*, O. Hobart Mowrer asks a penetrating question: "Has evangelical religion sold its birthright for a mess of psychological pottage?" [30] It's time for Christians to look objectively and prayerfully at the birthright and the mess of pottage.

Part Two

Mind / Body? . . . Body / Mind?

6. Intricate Interaction

The complexity of the human mind displays our Creator's remarkable ability not only to create one basic design, but also to cause each person to be particularly unique. Because of the complexity of God's design and the vast variety of individual differences, human knowledge of the mind and emotions is limited at best. As the research noted in the previous chapters indicates, there are more questions now than ever before about the effectiveness of psychotherapy, and there is considerable concern about its potential harm.

Besides the studies attempting to determine the results of psychotherapeutic treatment, researchers have also been investigating possible reasons for mental-emotional disorders. Two general groups of causes are the psychological and the biological, the first having to do with the mind and the second with the body. Furthermore, these are not mutually exclusive because of the intricate interaction between the physical and the mental-emotional aspects of a person.

To demonstrate the intimate relationship of the mind and body, we will first consider how the mind affects the body. Next, we will look at how the body affects the mind and examine some of the research findings on physical causes of mental-emotional disorders. Finally, we will discuss the inherent problems in misdiagnosis and mistreatment, which result from inadvisedly assuming psychological causes, rather than investigating the possibility of physical reasons for behavioral malfunctions.

7. *Mind / Body*

The complication of the close relationship between the mind and the body is demonstrated in the amazing placebo effect. In order to understand this surprising effect, imagine a person coming to a medical doctor with such symptoms as headaches and abdominal pains. After thoroughly examining the patient and finding nothing physically wrong, and after interviewing the patient and deciding that the symptoms may be a result of worry and stress, the doctor prescribes a dummy drug or placebo. The imitation drug is very often a milk-sugar tablet made to look like the real thing. The medicinal looking pill which has no curative power in itself may have a remarkable effect on the patient. Often the headaches cease and the abdominal pains disappear. This extraordinary reaction, called the *placebo effect*, is well known by doctors and is referred to in numerous medical studies. Frederick Evans says:

> The sensitive physician who is skillfully practicing the art of medicine will maximize the placebo effect, and thus help his patient at the minimum possible risk. Drugs such as morphine may be addicting. Sugar pills are not.[1]

Placebos have been shown to work for both physical and mental problems. Evans says with respect to physical problems, "Thus, a placebo cuts intense pain in half for about one suffering patient in three." He also says that one-third of the patients "will have their pain reduced equally well by both morphine and a placebo." [2] Additionally, patients suffering from mental disorders, such as depression, have shown improvement through the use of placebos. Some studies indicate that mildly depressed patients have shown the same improvement with placebos as with regular drugs.[3]

Although placebos have demonstrated their suggestive power in relieving symptoms in both emotional and physical disorders, they have not had the same effect in extreme mental-emotional disorders. According to the research, placebos are of no significant value in extreme cases.[4] This should not surprise us as those who have extreme disorders do not have the presence of mind to accept the power of suggestion that accompanies the fake pill and those who are chronically anxious may not be open to the suggestion of hope. After all, the placebo effect is not the power of a milk-sugar pill; it is the power of suggestion, accompanied by faith in the system or in the doctor administering the fake medicine.

Besides an element as simple as the placebo and its effect on both the body and the mind, there are a number of other mental-emotional factors which influence the condition of the body. One example of the strong influence of a person's emotions in the healing process of the body is that of laughter. Norman Cousins' own miraculous recovery from a serious disease of the connective tissue involved the use of humor and laughter. He found that "ten minutes of genuine belly laughter had an anesthetic effect and would give me at least two hours of pain-free sleep." Later he said, "I was greatly elated by the discovery that there is a physiologic basis for the ancient theory that laughter is good medicine." [5]

The relationship between body and mind and particularly the possible influence of the mental-emotional state on disease is being studied by a number of people. Medical doctors Meyer Friedman and Ray H. Rosenman in their book *Type A Behavior and Your Heart* relate personality and heart disease. They compare Type A people, who are competitive, aggressive, and hard-driving individuals, with Type B people, who are easy going. They found Type A people more prone to heart attack than Type B individuals. They assert, "We believe that the major cause of coronary artery and heart disease is a complex of emotional reactions, which we have designated Type A Behavior Pattern." [6]

They also investigated the relationship between cholesterol and behavior and conclude that "there is no question about the fact that the serum cholesterol level may vary directly with the intensity of the Type A Behavior Pattern." [7] Because of their observation concerning the relationship of the mental attitude and emotional pattern with the health of the heart, they proposed guidelines and suggestions for changing behavior to reduce the risk of heart disease.

Stress is definitely a factor which can affect the physical well-being of a person. There is a strong link between stress and illness. While it is not always apparent how it happens, studies clearly indicate that stress often leads to illness. It is even possible to predict illness based on the amount of stress in a person's life.[8] Although some stress is normal and natural, too much stress can cause havoc with the body.

Kenneth Pelletier in an article entitled "Mind as Healer, Mind as Slayer" reports, "Medical and psychological problems caused by stress have become the number-one health problem in the last decade. One standard medical text estimates that 50 to 80 percent of all diseases have their origins in stress."[9] In describing how stress can have such a powerful effect on the individual, Pelletier explains, "Stress can alter a person's brain-wave activity, endocrine and immunological balance, blood supply and pressure, respiration rate and pattern, and digestive processes."[10] In fact, James Hassett reports that about one-third of the adults in this country has high blood pressure and that "More than 90 percent of these cases are diagnosed as 'essential hypertension'—a euphemism that means nobody really knows what is causing it."[11]

Norman Cousins discusses the relationship between the mind and body in an article entitled "The Mysterious Placebo: How Mind Helps Medicine Work." He believes that the placebo effect proves that the mind and body are inseparable. He says:

> Attempts to treat most mental diseases as though they were completely free of physical causes and attempts to treat most bodily diseases as though the mind were in no way involved must be considered archaic in the light of new evidence about the way the human body functions.[12]

Mental-emotional factors can both aggravate and improve physical health. There is much support for both psychosomatic illness and psychosomatic health.

The interaction between the mind and the body raises a question of the "chicken and egg" variety. Which came first, the physical disease or the mental-emotional condition?

Which is the cause and which is the effect? Did the mind cause the body problem or is it the other way around? We need to be careful of the two extremes here. The one extreme is that all biological problems are due to psychological conditions and the other is that all mental problems are due to biological conditions.

8. *Body / Mind*

There is a delicate balance between the mental-emotional and the biological factors contributing to the condition of the total person. While less severe emotional disorders may be brought about by environmental and relationship factors, there is a strong indication that extreme mental-emotional problems are biological in origin.

As we look at such factors as heredity, physical disease, brain damage, brain disease, and biochemical theories, we will discover that certain mental-emotional disorders do have biological origins. As we examine some of these biologically caused disorders, we must question the value of psychotherapy as a means of cure. Furthermore, if some mental-emotional disorders are biologically caused, the question arises as to which ones and how many originate from biological factors.

These queries are important to consider because most people are not aware of recent research in this area and are still influenced by psychotherapeutic propaganda. They believe in the psychological origin of all mental-emotional disorders which have no obvious organic base, because they have been exposed to the apparent success of psychotherapy as portrayed in the media rather than the failures of psychotherapy as published in journals and books.

The romantic image of psychotherapy is a distortion frequently based upon fiction rather than fact. People would often rather believe an easily digested fabrication than a less palatable truth. The general public rarely reads the research and the media rarely reveals it. Therefore the romantic image of psychotherapy is out of phase with the results of research.

To examine what research does say about the possible biological causes of mental-emotional disorders, we need to consider the two main classes of disorders. The first is neurosis, which is now more commonly labeled *anxiety*. The second is psychosis, which is a label for several extreme mental-emotional disorders.

Here we will mainly examine the psychotic reactions, because these are the ones that help us focus on the biological versus the psychological causes and treatments. Also, the psychotic cases, because of their extremity, are far more easily identifiable than the neurotic.

Genetics

Genetics has been used to investigate the possible biological basis of some mental-emotional disorders. A number of studies have observed the relationship between schizophrenia and heredity. Schizophrenia, one of several psychotic disorders, is the most common diagnosis of hospitalized mental patients. If we can demonstrate that schizophrenia can be inherited, then we have established a genetic or biological cause for this psychotic disorder.

Numerous studies have been done on schizophrenic parents and their offspring. The various studies indicate that schizophrenia tends to be passed from parents to their children. In cases in which the children were raised in the same home as their schizophrenic parents, environmental factors could have contributed to the condition of the children, as well as the genetic factors. After all, parents do exert a psychological influence on their children, and children tend to model themselves after their parents.

However, further studies were made of children with schizophrenic parents in which the children had been placed in foster homes, either at birth or shortly thereafter. In such cases, researchers have the opportunity to see the effects of heredity outside the influence of an environment of schizophrenia. These studies even more dramatically emphasize the significance of heredity.

Barbara Fish in an editorial in the *American Journal of Psychiatry* remarked, "We are only beginning to comprehend how widespread the genetic influence of schizophrenia may be." [13]

Seymour S. Kety and his colleagues report, "The findings provide support for a theory of genetic transmission of vulnerability to schizophrenia, but they also imply the requirement of nongenetic, environmental factors for the development of clinical schizophrenic illness." [14]

In order to zero in on this heredity versus environment dilemma, research was conducted on identical and fraternal twins who were placed in foster homes. Generally speaking, identical twins are biologically the same while fraternal twins are like any other brothers and sisters in a family. Because of the biological similarity of identical twins, they should both inherit mental illness more often than both fraternal twins would. And, in fact, the research shows that schizophrenia is found significantly more often in both identical twins than in both fraternal twins. Incidence of fraternal twins inheriting schizophrenia is the same as that of sisters and brothers in the same family.

The environmental factors were removed when the identical twins were separated not only from their biological parents, but also from each other. In such cases the incidences of identical twins both inheriting schizophrenia were still higher than those of fraternal twins both having the same disorder. [15] Thus, the results generally indicate that whether ordinary children or identical twins remain in the same family as their schizophrenic parents or are placed in foster homes, *heredity is a significant factor in their future mental-emotional life.*

In a volume which reports on the studies of twins and genetic factors contributing to schizophrenia, the authors state that for a person to have true schizophrenia he must be genetically susceptible before environmental factors can seemingly bring on the disorder. [16] Another researcher, Leonard Heston, concludes from his extensive research in this area, "The importance of genetic factors in the development of schizophrenia has by now been established beyond reasonable dispute." [17]

Besides heredity being a causal factor in schizophrenia, research indicates that it is also an influencing factor in the manic-depressive and the psychotic depressive disorders. These disorders have been found to run in families, even when the children of disturbed parents have been adopted at birth.[18] Evidence also supports a genetic influence on some forms of neurosis, such as anxiety neurosis. After reviewing a wide range of research in this area, Gary Miner concluded that there are probably many genetic variations which may contribute to a biological predisposition to neurosis.[19]

How many other forms of mental-emotional disorders have some degree of origin in the genetic makeup of individuals is still unknown. However, the very fact of genetic factors predisposing persons to mental disorders indicates biological causation as a strong ingredient in the complex set of circumstances contributing to such disorders. It may be that just as some people are born with a tendency towards heart disease, cancer, diabetes, hypoglycemia, and so on, one might inherit physical impairment which may lead to mental-emotional disorders.

Other Biological Theories

Another area of investigation that has been helpful in understanding whether some mental-emotional disorders are biologically or psychologically caused is the study of the impact of bodily diseases on the mental life. All sorts of physical diseases can bring on mental-emotional problems. These diseases produce symptoms which would ordinarily be considered psychological rather than physical in origin.

Related to this idea is a theory that refers to brain damage which may occur during the prenatal period or during the birth process. The proponents of this theory suggest that a gradient of injury may occur, which at its worst would cause death at birth or shortly thereafter, but which would otherwise predispose a person to a variety of other possible malfunctions of the brain, including cerebral palsy, epilepsy, and mental-emotional disorders.[20]

Recent theories tend to indicate a biochemical basis for some mental-emotional disorders. According to the article "It's Not All in Your Head" by Seymour Kety, biochemical theories are not new. He said that the biochemical approach to mental disorders can be traced to a physician-biochemist nearly 100 years ago by the name of Thudichum, who hypothesized that toxic substances fermenting in the body brought on many forms of insanity. Such theories which existed at that time were overlooked in favor of psychoanalysis and other forms of psychotherapy.[21]

The use of recently discovered drugs to reduce symptoms of mental disorders inspired a renewed interest in the biochemical origins of mental-emotional problems. Kety observes, " . . . over the past two decades substantial indications have revealed that these serious mental illnesses have biochemical underpinnings." [22]

The effectiveness of drugs in alleviating some of the symptoms of schizophrenia, such as hearing voices and not being able to distinguish fact from fantasy, has been demonstrated both in and out of mental hospitals. Philip May, in his book *Treatment of Schizophrenia*, compared methods of treating schizophrenic patients and found that the use of drugs, primarily phenothiazines, was more effective in ameliorating the symptoms than psychotherapy, electric shock, non-treatment, or even the combination of psychotherapy and drugs.[23] Interestingly enough, May found that "psychotherapy alone appeared to have little effect or even a slightly adverse one" and that psychotherapy had little advantage over no treatment at all.[24]

Depression and manic-depressive psychosis also seem to respond positively to the use of drugs. Lithium is used as a form of maintenance treatment for a person suffering from manic-depressive psychosis. Although lithium does not cure the malady, it seems to stabilize the mind and reduce the symptoms as long as the patient continues the drug. The use of lithium for manic-depressives has been compared to the use of insulin by diabetics. Thus, the apparent usefulness of drugs suggests a biochemical problem in those suffering from manic-depressive psychosis, as well as in those suffering from schizophrenia.

While we have mentioned the use of drugs to suggest a biological basis for certain mental-emotional disorders, we are definitely not recommending drugs as a means of relieving or controlling behavior, because of the possibility of future damage. In fact, there seems to be an extreme over-ingestion of drugs by persons with psychiatric maladjustments.

Quite often these persons are taking what Frank Ayd, Jr., calls a "pharmacologic stew," which consists of "one or more neuroleptics, an antidepressant, an antiparkinsonian agent, one or more minor tranquilizers, a hypnotic, and possibly a psychostimulant." [25] Besides this, many people self-medicate with over-the-counter remedies, some of which counter side effects of the prescribed drugs. Additionally, an unknown number regularly indulge in alcohol. Another warning comes from Thomas Szasz: "You will see the day when the injuries caused by thorazine and lithium will be one of the major public health problems in this country." [26]

The only purpose in discussing the current use of drug therapy is to give some support to the biological rather than the psychological emphasis in determining possible causes of mental disorders, since popular opinion has been biased in favor of psychological, sociological, and environmental causes.

Further evidence to support the biochemical as well as biological theories regarding the cause of mental-emotional disorders has been set forth by Elliot Valenstein in an article titled "Science-Fiction Fantasy and the Brain." He reports that more is being learned about the biochemistry of brain circuits through a technique of brain-staining. Swedish researchers have identified a path of dopamine, which is a chemical substance which transmits impulses from one nerve to another.[27] The dopamine system helps regulate emotional arousal, and it appears that schizophrenics have an abnormally large number of dopamine receptors. Valenstein concludes:

> All of this evidence (and there is much more) suggests that there are dopamine circuits that play a crucial role in normal and abnormal behavior by adjusting the responsiveness of sensory-motor systems.[28]

Allergist Ben Feingold, in his book *Why Your Child Is Hyperactive*, proposes another biochemical explanation for abnormal behavior. He believes that salicylates, salicylate-related substances, and common food additives, such as artificial flavors and colors, can lead to behavioral changes.[29] K. E. Moyer reports that aggression can be an allergic response to pollens, drugs, or foods. Such allergens affect the nervous system and may bring on mild symptoms, such as irritability, to severe symptoms, such as psychotic aggressive reaction.[30]

There is a variety of other biological theories as to the possible cause of certain mental-emotional disorders. Some have suggested poor nutrition. Observations of the diets of schizophrenic patients have shown a high incidence of refined sugar, refined flour, and caffeinated beverages.[31] Besides nutrition, others have suggested that the cause could be inherited enzyme deficiencies. E. Fuller Torrey proposes environmental toxins, heavy metals, and certain viruses with long latency periods as possible causal factors in schizophrenia.[32] We have obviously not reached any definite conclusions regarding the real cause of mental disorders. However, it may be that there are multiple biological factors, each contributing to a form of emotional disorder.

A fairly extreme biological position regarding schizophrenia is taken by a number of researchers, including Torrey, who is a psychiatrist doing research on immunological abnormalities in schizophrenics. After mentioning several myths of schizophrenia in his article "Schizophrenia: Sense and Nonsense," he declares, "For schizophrenia is most certainly a brain disease—the evidence has become overwhelming on that point." By brain disease he means *organic* brain disease. He goes on to say, "The part of the brain that is diseased appears to be the limbic system and/or the upper portion of the brain stem." [33]

Techniques of psychotherapy have been so highly esteemed because of the claims of psychotherapists and their clients' subjective testimonials that they continue to be perpetrated as the primary cure for mental-emotional disorders. Meltzoff and Kornreich declare:

> The therapeutic literature abounds in testimonials illustrated by carefully selected, wondrous case reports that boggle the eye and captivate the imagination.[34]

In spite of the research, there continues to be a simplistic and dishonest representation of psychotherapy. Psychotherapists generally ignore the body/mind relationship and, according to Torrey, "still treat schizophrenia with psychotherapy and psychoanalysis, although those treatments have been largely discredited in the rest of the world." [35] Torrey contends that "there is not one shred of scientific evidence that psychological experiences (early childhood or otherwise) cause true schizophrenia, or that any true schizophrenic has ever been talked out of the disease." [36]

While a variety of studies have been done on the relationship between the biological and mental-emotional disorders with varying results, there appears to be more support now than ever before for the biological theories. We know that there are biological causes of some mental-emotional disorders, but we do not know if they are the only causes, the primary causes, or several of many contributing factors. Research indicates that biological factors are involved: the amount of involvement is yet to be determined.

This kind of research should at least lead us to question the generally accepted image of the psychological origin of mental-emotional disorders, even when no apparent organic cause is evident.

9. Body / Mind: Misdiagnosis and Mistreatment

The intimate relationship between the body and the mind has led to misunderstanding and misdiagnosis during the entire history of psychotherapy. The problem of biological disorders that were thought to be psychological problems and treated as such is a grim skeleton in the therapeutic closet. Most psychotherapists would like to ignore or forget about this history of looking at and treating psychological symptoms which were really the result of physical diseases.

At one time in this history there were physical diseases which were considered to be mental disorders because of the accompanying mental symptoms. Two examples are general paresis, caused by the spirochete of syphilis invading the brain, and pellagrous psychosis, caused by a dietary deficiency of nicotinic acid. In both cases numerous people who have suffered from these diseases were labeled schizophrenic and treated accordingly. The following account is just one of many case histories involving misdiagnosis.

A twenty-two-year-old woman exhibited certain symptoms similar to those of schizophrenia. Rather than suggesting a comprehensive physical, the psychiatrist to whom she was referred diagnosed her condition as schizophrenic and treated her accordingly. However, it was later discovered that her depression and hallucinations were due to pellagrous psychosis, which had been brought on by a crash diet and near starvation conditions.[37]

Sending a person to a mental institution instead of treating the physical problem not only prevents possible cure, but also adds even more horror to the agony of the disease itself. Can you imagine the number of people who have suffered from such physical diseases and were treated as insane because of ignorance of the real problem? Even Parkinson's disease was once considered a mental disorder and treated by means of psychotherapy.

This raises the whole problem of misdiagnosis and the tendency to refer people to psychotherapists. There have been and still are great numbers of individuals erroneously referred to psychotherapy who are really suffering from physical disorders. A number of people, whose neurotic and psychotic behavior has been caused by low blood sugar, have been treated by psychotherapy because the disorder was not recognized as hypoglycemia. One twenty-six-year-old woman suffered from symptoms of depression and anxiety. For an entire year before a doctor properly diagnosed her condition as hypoglycemia, she had been taking tranquilizers and seeing a psychotherapist on a regular basis. Furthermore, she had been hospitalized twice because of persistent suicidal thoughts.[38]

Allen Bergin in an article "Psychotherapy Can Be Dangerous" mentions a female patient who had several physical problems and was being treated by a psychotherapist. He reports, "Although he had an M.D., he never suggested a physical examination. A subsequent medical exam revealed she was suffering from anemia and low metabolism."[39]

Another example of misdiagnosis, mistreatment, and the

accompanying nightmare is found in neurosurgeon I. S. Cooper's book *The Victim Is Always the Same*.[40] One of the most pathetic parts of the book has to do with two little girls who had the rare disease dystonia, which is a neurological disease involving involuntary muscular movements mainly of the arms and legs. Before it was finally discovered that they were actually suffering from dystonia, the girls and their parents went through almost endless psychotherapeutic terror, all in the name of diagnosis, treatment, and help.

All the doctors and social workers involved thought only of psychological factors as they observed the overt symptoms, which consisted of strange movements while walking and odd, disconnected arm movements. These symptoms were regarded by the professionals as bizarre behavior, which they felt indicated that the girls were emotionally disturbed and were symbolically acting out inner struggle and anxiety. Through the various interviews, the parents were regarded as neurotic, distressed, and anxious. No one evidently stopped to consider that these parents were naturally concerned about their children and the diagnoses which they were hearing.

Both parents and girls underwent weeks and months of individual psychotherapy and group therapy, and one of the girls was even admitted to a psychiatric hospital. The more the symptoms persisted, the more the professionals told the parents that they were not cooperating and that there was resistance to therapy. One child went through the agony of being interviewed in front of television cameras and in front of other doctors and, worst of all, she was not allowed to see her parents, who, it was thought, might ruin the therapy with their own presence.

At last, quite by accident, one of the neurologists in the hospital happened to notice the child in passing and identified what she had—dystonia. Throughout this entire period of time, Cooper reports, the psychiatrists, psychologists, social workers, and group therapists demonstrated an astonishing amount of self-confidence in what they were doing. One might wonder about how much psychological damage they bestowed in the name of therapy.

Although this seems to be an isolated story, it is not at all unusual. In an article entitled "Dystonia: A Disorder Often Misdiagnosed as a Conversion Reaction," neurologists Ronald P. Lesser and Stanley Fahn state that from the records of 84 patients who actually had dystonia 37 had been originally diagnosed as mentally ill. They report, "These patients had received without benefit a variety of psychiatric therapies, including psychoanalysis for up to 2 years, psychoanalytic psychotherapy, behavioral therapy, hypnosis, and pharmacotherapy." [41]

The preceding cases are only examples of what can happen in this whole gray area of body/mind. Many persons have been given psychotherapeutic treatment without success and were even hospitalized because they were suffering from some physical disease or from inherited disorders like dystonia. The tragedy of it all continues even today.

10. Mind, Body, or the Whole Man?

The brain is obviously central to the mind-body relationship because it controls every organ system in the body. In addition, the brain also responds to every organ system within the body. This interaction of body to mind and mind to body is a complex process, and the enigma of it prevents us from knowing much truth about the underlying causes of human behavior. Our knowledge is limited because the secrets of human behavior are locked up in the mind-body relationship and particularly in the brain. Michael Chase, in an article entitled "The Matriculating Brain," wrote, "The human brain, for all our intimacy with it, has surrendered less to scientific research than have the distant moon, stars and ocean floor, or such intimate processes as genetic coding, immune reactions or muscle contraction." [42]

There has been an unfortunate division of mind and body. What generally happens is that the medical doctor's main interest is with the body and the psychotherapist's with the mind. The separation of mind from body is a naive way of dealing with the total person. In fact, the total person also includes the spirit. The body, mind and the spirit must be considered in any problem which a person is experiencing. Man is a whole being, made up of a complex combination of body, mind, and spirit. Any system which regards one, such as the body or the mind, without considering all three, and particularly the spiritual part of man, falls short of truly ministering to the whole person.

Part Three

Psychotherapy: Questions, Critiques, Criticisms

11. Science or Pseudoscience?

Psychotherapists claim to provide advantageous behavioral patterns for daily living, new awareness of the possibilities for selfhood, and adjustment to life and circumstances. They attempt to deal with such internal phenomena as thoughts, fears, and anxiety and with such outward behavior as social interaction, withdrawal, and aggression. In attempting to assess behavior and bring about changes, psychotherapy is swathed in subjectivity. Yet, its proponents call it scientific and dress it in medical terminology. Then, staged as a science and costumed in the garb of medicine, psychotherapy unabashedly performs according to personal interpretation, influenced by the many, often conflicting theoretical systems.

Is psychotherapy science or superstition? Is it objective or subjective? Is it fact or fabrication? Such questions are important because we have learned to trust almost anything labeled *science*. Our society has a penchant for science, for it has lifted us out of the ordinary and taken us to the moon and even helped us explore the distant planets. We have been impressed, surprised, and even awed in the twentieth century by the wonders of science. Science and its accompanying technology have propelled us towards a more comfortable way of life, although not necessarily towards a peaceful state of mind.

Science has made us feel knowledgeable, for it has enabled us to discover and describe many of the natural, physical laws of the universe. Likewise, we are anxious to have similar laws to describe the mental-emotional-behavioral makeup of man. Therefore, because psychotherapy has identified itself with the science of medicine and has been labeled a *behavioral science*, we consider it scientific in describing, analyzing, and treating the human condition.

If, indeed, psychology and psychotherapy are scientific, they will command our respect and attention. However, if they are not, we have reason to question and to doubt their bold assertions and methods. We tend to equate the word *scientific* with such concepts as truthfulness, accuracy, and reliability. Therefore, although many disciplines outside the realm of science may fascinate and attract us, they do not command our corporate confidence the way science does.

Since psychotherapy is based on the principles of psychology, it would be reasonable to ask if psychology itself can be considered a science. In attempting to evaluate the status of psychology, the American Psychological Association appointed Sigmund Koch to plan and direct a study which was subsidized by the National Science Foundation. This study involved eighty eminent scholars in assessing the facts, theories, and methods of psychology. The results of this extensive endeavor were then published in a seven volume series entitled *Psychology: A Study of a Science*.[1]

After examining the results, Koch concludes, "I think it by this time utterly and finally clear that *psychology cannot be a coherent science*." [2] (Italics his.) He further declares that such activities as perception, motivation, social psychology, psychopathology, and creativity cannot properly be labeled "science." [3] He suggests, "As the beginning of a therapeutic humility, we might re-christen *psychology* and speak instead of *the psychological studies*." [4] (Italics his.)

Sigmund Koch describes the delusion from which we have been suffering in thinking about psychology as a science.

> The *hope* of a psychological science became indistinguishable from the *fact* of psychological science. The entire subsequent history of psychology can be seen as a ritualistic endeavor to emulate the forms of science in order to sustain the delusion that it already *is* a science.[5] (Italics his.)

If psychology "cannot be a coherent science," neither can

psychotherapy, which rests upon psychological foundations. One reason why psychotherapy cannot legitimately be called a coherent science is because it treats human beings which are not only unique but possess a free will. Furthermore, the therapist and patient are each individually unique and their interaction lends an additional dimension of variability. When one adds time and changing circumstances, it is no wonder that the therapeutic relationship escapes the rigors of science.

In commenting on the uniqueness of humanity, Gordon Allport says that "it is a universally true statement, and therefore a law, that the personal patterns of individuality are unique." [6] In considering the dilemma between science and personal individuality, he states:

> The individual, whatever else he may be, is an internally consistent and unique organization of bodily and mental processes. But since he is unique, science finds him an embarrassment. Science, it is said, deals only with broad, preferably universal, laws. . . . Individuality cannot be studied by science, but only by history, art, or biography. [7]

We might further add, the individual not only escapes the formulas of science but even defies the descriptions of literature. However, if one must choose between the two, it seems that literature has more ably revealed man. It is language, not formulas, that best describes man. Language and literature, not personality theories and psychotherapy, can best portray man and provide a glimpse into the depths of his soul.

Prediction

One of the main failures of psychotherapy as a science is in the area of prediction. In physics and chemistry we can predict what will happen under given circumstances. We can even talk about the probability of certain events occurring. However, in psychotherapy the system breaks down at the level of prediction. We do not know why some people get better and some worse; we cannot even predict which ones will get better and which ones will deteriorate.

Much research on clinical judgment and decision-making reveals that the experts lack substantially in the ability to predict. Einhorn and Hogarth state that "it is apparent that neither the extent of professional training and experience nor the amount of information available to clinicians necessarily increases predictive accuracy." [8] The shocking thing about all this, the researchers point out, is that in spite of the great fallibility in professional judgment people seem to have unshakable confidence in it.

To circumvent this problem of prediction, some have called psychotherapy a *post-dictive science* rather than a *predictive science*. One psychologist admits, "Since the days of Freud, we have had to rely on post-dictive theories—that is, we have used our theoretical systems to explain or rationalize what has gone on before." [9] Thus, psychotherapists cannot predict the future mental-emotional health of their clients with any confidence. They can merely look into a person's past and guess how he got that way. Psychotherapy should not even be labeled *post-dictive* because the explanation of behavior and its relationship to the past is subjective and interpretive rather than objective and reliable.

Does Research Make Psychotherapy a Science?

A further confusion about psychotherapy and science has to do with the use of scientific research methods to investigate the success or failure of a given theory or treatment procedure. Some people assume that psychotherapy is a science because of the research conducted in the field. While it is true that research employs scientific methods, it does not follow that whatever is being investigated is scientific. Many nonscientific and even questionable practices, such as E.S.P., biorhythms, fingertip reading, and psychic phenomena a la Uri Geller, are being investigated by scientific research procedures. The scientific method has been used to investigate everything from art to Zen and from prayer to politics. We certainly would not call all of these "science."

Theory and Fact

Bertrand Russell once said, "Science, ever since the time of the Arabs, has had two functions: (1) to enable us to *know* things, and (2) to enable us to *do* things." [10]

Can psychotherapy qualify as a science in terms of what it does? Does psychotherapy enable us to know and to do? If we translate "knowing" into facts and "doing" into treatment, we can determine the scientific status of psychotherapy. The effectiveness of psychotherapeutic treatment was already discussed in Part One. Whether it works, how well it works, and how much it harms are open to question. Now let us look at the facts and theories of psychotherapy.

One major distinction between psychotherapy and science is the development and support of their respective theories. Scientific theories arrange observable, objective, verifiable facts into causal relationships.[11] Psychotherapeutic theories and personality theories, on the other hand, organize and suggest causal relationships of subjective ideas, insights, and intuition.

This question of scientific and pseudoscientific theories intrigued Karl Popper, who is considered one of the most influential thinkers of our day. As he investigated the differences between physical theories, such as Newton's theory of gravity and Einstein's theory of relativity, and theories about the behavior of men, he began to feel that Freud's theory of psychoanalysis and Adler's theory of individual psychology could not truly be considered scientific.[12]

Although such theories seem to be able to explain or interpret behavior, they rely on subjective interpretations. Even the claims of clinical observation cannot be considered objective or scientific since they are merely interpretations based on the theories familiar to the observer.[13] These theories depend upon confirmation rather than testability. If one is looking for verifications or confirmations, he'll find them with either theory. But, if he is trying to test a theory he will try to disprove it.

Popper says, "Every genuine *test* of a theory is an attempt to falsify it, or to refute it." [14] (Italics his.) For instance, if a person is test driving a newly designed car, he will not just drive it on a smooth road to verify that it works. He will also drive it under adverse conditions and test it to see what does not work. He will actually try to discover what, if anything, is wrong with it rather than just what is right. Popper declares,

"Confirming evidence should not count *except when it is the result of a genuine test of the theory*." [15] (Italics his.)

Furthermore, Popper believes that the theories formulated by Freud and Adler, "though posing as sciences, had in fact more in common with primitive myths than with science; that they resembled astrology rather than astronomy." [16] He also says, "These theories describe some facts, but in the manner of myths. They contain most interesting psychological suggestions, but not in a testable form." [17] Jerome Frank also refers to psychotherapies as psychotherapeutic myths because "they are not subject to disproof." [18] E. Fuller Torrey in his book *The Mind Game* seems to concur by saying, "The techniques used by Western psychiatrists are, with few exceptions, on exactly the same scientific plane as the techniques used by witch doctors." [19]

The idea that psychotherapists know a lot about human behavior is also a myth. To be perfectly honest, they know very little and have proven even less. Robert Rosenthal says, "But for all the centuries of effort, there is no compelling evidence to convince us that we do understand human behavior very well." [20] Explanations of human behavior include almost entirely unverifiable theories based upon introspection, interpretation, and imagination.

Men have developed numerous subjective theories with very little factual support. The varieties of these theories include the analytic, psychoanalytic, social psychological, field, constitutional, self, and so forth. Within these theories are other theories about such themes as infantile sexuality, the unconscious, dreams, and motivation. One might think that these theories would constitute a body of knowledge. However, personality theories and their psychotherapeutic counterparts do not fit together, for they often conflict with one another in both principle and application, as well as in terminology.

Sigmund Koch contends that psychology is not a cumulative or progressive discipline in which knowledge is added to knowledge. Rather, what is discovered by one generation "typically disenfranchises the theoretical fictions of the past." Instead of refining and specifying larger generalizations of the past, psychologists are busy replacing them. Koch declares, "Throughout psychology's history as 'science,' the *hard* knowledge it has deposited has been uniformly negative." [21] (Italics his.)

Creators of these theoretical explanations have become infatuated and puffed up with their innovative schemes as if these theories constitute reality, when, in fact, each theory only constitutes one man's impression of reality, which others have accepted. These theories only amount to ideas and beliefs *about* reality rather than to reality itself. They are only imaginative suppositions, *not* proven facts.

Learning theories about human behavior and personality is vastly different from knowing facts. For too long we have believed these theories to be factual. We need to stay out of the morass of opinions, contradictions, and unproven conceptions. We must stop speaking of these theories as if they represent reality and, worse yet, acting as if they are true. We need to recognize that there is much subjectivity, sentimentality, superstition, and even shamanism within this theoretical sand castle.

Take any text on behavior or personality or psychotherapy and examine it to see how much is subjective theory and how little is objective fact. Then remove all the pages that contain theories and see what remains. In most cases there would be almost nothing left. We are not saying that psychotherapeutic theories are intentionally dishonest, deceitful, or untruthful; we are merely pointing out a common error in thinking. Psychotherapy is not a coherent science, but a discipline based upon many theories and few verifiable facts.

Besides the confusion between theory and fact, notice that psychotherapeutic theories invariably cover the deepest and most profound levels of human behavior, while psychotherapeutic facts reveal the most superficial. Verifiable facts are not only few and far between; they cover only the most obvious aspects of man. Often they sound a little ridiculous. For example, a fact of human behavior would be something like this: men communicate with one another through language.

The deeper a person plunges into the psyche of man, the more theoretical he becomes. Then in order to explain these deep levels, the psychotherapist uses a mumbo jumbo of jargon and metaphors, of psychotherapeutic language and symbols. Nevertheless, we may feel comfortable with personality and psychotherapeutic theories because they *seem* to explain or categorize behavior. But, just because we feel comfortable does not mean that the theories are verifiable through objective, scientific testing. Perhaps we like theories because they help us organize our attitudes and easily explain away behavioral traits and actions.

Being confronted by human behavior without a frame of reference makes one feel insecure. Jerome Frank points out, "The first step to gaining control of any phenomenon is to give it a name." [22] Also, he says that we "need to master some conceptual framework to enable us to . . . maintain our own confidence." [23] We need names; we need words and thoughts. We need a Rosetta Stone to decipher the mysterious symbols and actions of the human psyche.

Without these we feel weak, ineffective, and impotent; but with psychotherapeutic theories we sense stability, direction, and power. We both desire and require theories to fulfill the need to grasp and make sense out of what we see and experience; without them we feel helpless. Thus, man invents and manipulates symbols for his own security and then believes and acts upon them as though they were reality.

However, we have no reason to feel powerful just because aspects of human behavior have been named, described and categorized. Naming and describing human behavior does not necessarily bring knowledge and understanding. There is a great gulf between talking about human behavior and changing it. Psychotherapeutic theory is merely a combination of subjective, yet scientific-sounding words. Karl Menninger once said, "But schizophrenia to me is just a nice Greek word that some psychiatrists use to sound scientific and impress relatives." [24] Many of these theories have a vacant and vacuous sounding vocabulary that defies description and definition. Yet, we are seduced by a scientific-sounding psychotherapeutic system which is sometimes just "a tale told by an idiot, full of sound and fury, signifying nothing." (*Macbeth*, Act V, Scene V)

12. Medical Model and Mental Illness

Quite often people refer to what is called the medical model in order to justify the use of psychotherapy. In using the medical model, they assume that mental illness can be thought of and talked about in the same manner and terms as medical illness. After all, these people reason, both are called "illnesses."

In the medical model physical symptoms are caused by some pathogenic agent. For example, a fever may be caused by viruses; remove the pathogenic agent and you remove the symptom. Or, a person may have a broken leg; set the leg according to learned techniques and the leg will heal. We have confidence in this model because it has worked well in the treatment of physical ailments. With the easy transfer of the model from the medical world to the psychotherapeutic world, many people believe that mental problems are the same as physical problems.

Applying the medical model to psychotherapy came from the relationship between psychiatry and medicine. Since psychiatrists are medical doctors and since psychiatry is a medical specialty, it seemed to follow that the medical model applied to psychiatry just as it did to medicine. Furthermore, psychiatry is draped with such medical trimmings as offices in medical clinics, hospitalization of patients, diagnostic services, prescription drugs, and therapeutic treatment. The very word *therapy* implies medical treatment. Further expansion of the use of the medical model to all of psychotherapy was easy after that.

The practice of medicine deals with the physical, biological aspects of a person; psychotherapy deals with the social, mental, and emotional aspects. Whereas medical doctors attempt to heal the body, psychotherapists attempt to alleviate or cure emotional, mental, and even spiritual suffering and to establish new patterns of social behavior. In spite of such differences, the medical model continues to be called upon to support the activities of the psychotherapist.

Additionally, the medical model supports the idea that a person with social or mental problems is ill. And with much sympathy we label people *mentally ill* and we categorize all mental problems under the key term *mental illness*. Thomas Szasz explains it this way:

If we now classify certain forms of personal conduct as illness, it is because most people believe that the best way to deal with them is by responding to them as if they were medical diseases.[25]

People believe this because they have been influenced by the medical model and are confused by the terminology. They think that if one can have a sick body, it must follow that one can have a sick mind. But, is the mind part of the body? Or can we equate the mind with the body? The authors of *The Madness Establishment* say, "Unlike many medical diseases that have scientifically verifiable etiologies and prescribed methods of treatment, most of the 'mental illnesses' have neither scientifically established causes nor treatments of proven efficacy." [26]

Psychotherapy deals with thoughts, emotions, and behavior, but not with the brain itself. Psychotherapy does not deal with the biology of the brain, but with the psychology of the mind and with the social behavior of the individual. In medicine we understand what a diseased body is, but what is the parallel in psychotherapy? It is obvious that in psychotherapy mental illness does not mean brain disease. If brain disease were the case, the person would be a *medical* patient, not a *mental* patient. Szasz very sharply refers to the "psychiatric imposter" who "supports a common, culturally shared desire to equate and confuse brain and mind, nerves and nervousness." [27] It is necessary to understand this distinction to appreciate the difference.

The assumption that medical illness and mental illness are alike is further dealt with by Szasz in his book *The Myth of Mental Illness*. He says:

It is customary to define psychiatry as a medical specialty concerned with the study, diagnosis, and treatment of mental illnesses. This is a worthless and misleading definition. Mental illness is a myth.

He continues:

I have argued that, today, the notion of a person "having a mental illness" is scientifically crippling. It provides professional assent to a popular rationalization—namely, that problems in living experienced and expressed in terms of so-called psychiatric symptoms are basically similar to bodily diseases.[28]

Although one may result from the other, *medical illness* and *mental illness* are simply not the same. *Biological* and *psychological* are not synonymous. One has to do with the organic processes and the other with the thought and emotional life. We should have rejected the word *illness* after the word *mental* from the very beginning.

The use of the medical model in psychotherapy does not reveal truth; instead it merely disguises psychotherapy with the mask of medical terminology and ends up confusing everyone. E. Fuller Torrey says:

> . . . the medical model of human behavior, when carried to its logical conclusions, is both nonsensical and nonfunctional. It doesn't answer the questions which are asked of it, it doesn't provide good service, and it leads to a stream of absurdities worthy of a Roman circus.[29]

The error of applying medical terminology to mental life causes erroneous thinking and responding. The very word *medical* carries with it the suggested treatment, for if we are dealing with an illness, medical treatment is implied. Therefore, whenever someone suggests that you should believe in psychotherapy because you believe in medicine, remember that medical illness and mental illness are *not* the same.

13. *Diagnostic Confusion*

One more area of investigation is that of diagnosis. Since one property of a science is that it provides a valid means of measurement, it seems reasonable to ask the following question. Do psychotherapeutic theories and techniques enable one to accurately determine the mental-emotional state of an individual through either diagnostic testing or personal interview?

Diagnostic Testing

A number of diagnostic tests have been developed and used by psychotherapists. Many people consider that because these are tests, they are scientific and therefore accurate. But are they accurate and do they lend some credibility to psychotherapy as a science? We tend to think of a test as being an objective instrument which gives true information about individuals. This is a generalization that does not apply to all tests and particularly does not apply to tests used by psychotherapists.

The most important question about any test is its validity. The validity of a test is its integrity; that is, does the test measure what it says it measures or does it reveal what it claims to reveal? In simple language, does the test do what it says it does? Does a test of typing speed actually measure a person's typing speed? Does an arithmetic achievement test measure the person's achievement in arithmetic? Does a test of emotional stability actually measure that stability?

As we measure different levels of human behavior and personality by tests, we find that the more superficial the quality measured, the higher the integrity of the test. Conversely, the deeper the quality measured, the lower the integrity. Tests of performance, such as typing and finger dexterity, have a high degree of integrity, while tests of personality have low degrees of integrity. The most superficial aspects of behavior can usually be tested fairly accurately, whereas the deepest layers of our personality do not lend themselves well to testing.

Unfortunately, we seem to place performance testing and personality testing in the same category and have confidence in both. Since we have taken tests in school and have been led to believe that a test is a test is a test, we do not discriminate as we should. Some tests can be trusted but others cannot. There is a high probability of poor integrity for personality tests.

Psychotherapists often rely on personality tests in diagnosing and treating their clients. These tests are called personality inventories and projective techniques. Projective techniques, such as the Rorschach and the Thematic Apperception Test, present visual images or pictures which are ambiguous in meaning so that the person taking the test has a wide range of possible subjective responses, which supposedly reveal his inner self.

Personality tests lend themselves to many kinds of distortions. Besides the subjective nature of the test itself, the person evaluating the responses may unintentionally influence his appraisal with aspects of his own personality, biases, and preconceived ideas of the examinee. His evaluation may be based on social-financial, educational, cultural, or physical aspects rather than on the person's mental-emotional condition. Furthermore, subtleties in the interaction between the examiner and the examinee may influence responses. In fact, the sex of the examiner has been shown to influence the responses of women who have taken the Rorschach.[30]

One experiment involving the use of projective devices was conducted in which experienced clinicians were asked to differentiate the responses of several types of people, including anxiety neurotics, paranoid schizophrenics, depressives, and adult imbeciles. According to Richard Stuart's report in *Trick or Treatment: How and When Psychotherapy Fails*,

> The judges succeeded in differentiating the responses of the adult imbeciles but were right only half of the time with the remaining patients.[31]

Thus, besides the notoriously poor integrity of the tests themselves, the psychotherapists may compound the problem through misinterpretation and erroneous conclusions.

Because of this poor integrity and the subjectivity involved in evaluating the responses, we should look with suspicion and view with distrust the varying conclusions and revelations that proceed from the mouths of psychotherapists based upon the use of such tests. K. B. Little reports that, even at their best, predictions based on the use of projective devices are "largely a waste of time." [32] Szasz warns:

> In more than twenty years of psychiatric work, I have never known a clinical psychologist to report, on the basis of a projective test, that the subject is a "normal, mentally healthy person." While some witches may have survived dunking, no "madman" survives psychological testing . . . there is no behavior or person that a modern psychiatrist cannot plausibly diagnose as abnormal or ill.[33]

The best-known and most idolized projective technique is the Rorschach inkblot test. It has been in use for over fifty years and was developed by Hermann Rorschach, a Swiss psychiatrist. The test provides ten cards, each with a bilaterally symmetrical inkblot on it. Five of these cards are in black and white, and the other five are colored. An examiner shows these cards to a person and asks him to describe what he sees. The examiner then evaluates the responses of the individual.

Religious symbols mentioned during a Rorschach test will generally be scored as abnormal responses. In the book *Rorschach Interpretation: Advanced Technique*, the authors state:

> Religion contents are virtually never present in the records of normals. Their occurrence is associated with profound concern about the problems of good and evil, concern which, almost always, is a screen for and displacement of guilt induced by sexual preoccupation. Religion contents may be used to infer critical and unresolved problems of sexuality. . . . [Religion] responses are most common among schizophrenics, particularly patients with delusions which concern religion.[34]

It would be interesting to discover how many unsuspecting Christians have taken the Rorschach test and been thus "treated" for sexual preoccupation.

Everyone seems to know about this supposedly "magical" instrument, but few question its value. During the mid-sixties at least one million people per year took the test. This required about five million hours of administering and scoring at a grand take of $25,000,000 per year.[35] While there has been a slight decline, the Rorschach continues to be given about a million times a year and with inflation the total cost is no doubt higher than in the sixties.[36]

Even though psychotherapists are aware of the studies that reveal the poor integrity of the test, they continue to use it, hoping to discover at least one hidden clue to the meaning of a person. And yet, what do they really discover? Are they finding hidden treasure or is that treasure as elusive as the pot of gold? In claiming to measure or at least reveal the deepest levels of personality, the Rorschach has not even given us the ability to distinguish fool's gold from the real thing.

Arthur Jensen summarizes the status of the Rorschach test in the *Mental Measurements Yearbook*.

> Put frankly, the consensus of qualified judgment is that the Rorschach is a very poor test and has no practical worth for any of the purposes for which it is recommended by its devotees.[37]

The Rorschach and other personality tests of poor integrity have been used far too long. Yet, it will be an even longer time before they are abandoned. As long as astrological charts, biorhythmic calendars, and mantras remain popular, the

Rorschach and similar tests will retain their mystique.

Diagnostic Interviews

Diagnostic testing has low validity because of the subjective nature of the tests and the possible misinterpretation by the examiner. Personal interviews lack validity for the same reasons. Diagnostic interviews are vulnerable to the many possibilities of miscommunication, preconceived ideas, and distorted or self-conscious responses to such an artificial situation.

A psychotherapeutic diagnosis is generally the final product of a process of what is called *clinical judgment,* and quite often only one person makes the judgment. Yet, one therapist may view a particular individual as relatively healthy and well adjusted, while another may view the same person as deeply disturbed.[38] A client seeking help may also respond entirely differently to a variety of interviewers, depending on the personality of each. Furthermore, there is no agreed upon definitions of many psychological terms such as *emotional stability* or *instability* and *normality* or *abnormality.* Thus the question of validity is meaningless almost from the start.

The subjective nature of diagnosing by interview involves certain characteristics of the client and of the interviewer. Since the interview is an interpersonal process, extraneous characteristics of the client may influence the final judgment. Some of the factors found to distort the evaluation are: the socio-economic status of the client, with lower-class persons more likely to be diagnosed as severely disturbed than middle-class persons; personality similarities between client and interviewer; the attitude of the person towards the interview and the psychotherapist; the physical characteristics of the client; the strain of being interviewed; and the mood of the client that particular day.[39]

Individual characteristics of the interviewer may also distort the final diagnosis in the following ways. Each interviewer has certain expectations concerning responses and will sometimes in very subtle, unintentional ways elicit certain responses to his questions. Interviewers may ask leading questions related to their own theoretical orientations and interests and may gear the entire interview in these directions, thus missing a great deal of balancing responses. Even if they are careful to avoid leading questions, they may nevertheless interpret every response according to their own theoretical bias.

Other errors may come from inaccurate observation, poor reasoning, personal biases, misinterpretation of behavior, seeming similarities between clients, and even the interviewer's current mood, mental health, and physical condition.[40]

With this vast array of possible interferences and mistakes, it is amazing that psychotherapists can feel so confident in their diagnoses. And it is likewise amazing that the public so readily receives the labels that follow the diagnosis. Labels such as *manic-depressive, schizophrenic, psychotic,* and *neurotic* severely influence the lives of those who have been branded *mentally ill.*

A number of studies have been made in which clients have been interviewed and diagnosed by both professionals and nonprofessionals. In fourteen studies which compared the diagnostic accuracy of psychologists and nonpsychologists, six studies indicated no differences in the amount of accuracy between the two groups. Five studies indicated greater reliability in the psychologists' evaluations, but three studies revealed that nonpsychologists were better at diagnosing.[41] Another study showed that physical scientists outranked psychologists in making psychotherapeutic diagnoses and yet another indicated that Protestant housewives outperformed the professionals.[42]

Distinguishing the Sane from the Insane

If psychotherapy were a science, there would be a reliable, objective and accurate means of at least distinguishing the sane from the insane. David Rosenhan from Stanford University conducted a unique and interesting experiment related to this question. In the experiment eight sane volunteers, including Rosenhan, three psychologists, one pediatrician, one housewife, and a painter, gained admission to twelve mental hospitals by complaining that they had been hearing voices.

Aside from the limited fake symptoms, pseudonyms, and fictitious occupations on the part of those whose occupations might otherwise attract attention, the volunteers presented themselves honestly. Actual family, work, and school relationships were shared, and both positive and negative feelings were described. Thus, aside from a small identity cover up and initial fake symptoms, the pseudopatients behaved and shared themselves as they really were. In fact, it was up to each volunteer to convince the staff that he was sane enough to be released; thus they were strongly motivated to exhibit model behavior to earn discharge as soon as possible.[43]

Although staff reports on the pseudopatients included remarks such as "friendly," "cooperative," and "exhibited no abnormal indication," the hospital staffs, including psychiatrists, nurses, and attendants, uniformly failed to detect sanity among the fake patients, who acted and spoke normally. Some of the real patients, on the other hand, were suspicious. Rosenhan reported that when they were initially keeping accurate records 35 out of 118 patients verbalized their suspicions. They even suggested that the pseudopatients were journalists or professors investigating the hospital.[44]

The hospital staff, on the other hand, viewed the patients through the labels of the initial diagnosis so that all subsequent actions and words were seen in the context of that distorted conceptual image. The pseudopatients wrote daily observations about the activities at the hospital. At first they did it in secret. Then later, since it was obvious that no one on the staff suspected anything, they wrote their notes openly. The staff merely regarded the note-taking as part of their disturbed conduct, symptoms of delusions or compulsive behavior. Other normal actions were sometimes misunderstood in terms of the initial diagnosis. When a nurse saw one volunteer pacing the halls, she asked if he was nervous; his complaint was that he was bored.[45]

Besides not recognizing their sanity at admission and through their stay, the staff also failed to recognize their sanity when they were discharged. In eleven of the twelve hospitals, the pseudopatients were admitted with a diagnosis of schizophrenia and then later discharged with a diagnosis of schizophrenia "in remission." In the twelfth case, the diagnosis was manic-depressive psychosis in both admission and discharge.[46] One might excuse such gross oversights in below-average hospitals, but Rosenhan assures us that three of the twelve were top ranking and had AMA approved residency programs.[47]

Rosenhan suggests that perhaps one reason why the psychiatrists and nurses failed to detect sanity was because of caution. Perhaps they feared misdiagnosing in the direction of sanity more than in the direction of insanity. Therefore, he decided to perform a follow-up experiment with a reverse twist. He chose a research and teaching hospital in which the staff was familiar with the results of the previous study and had boasted that they would have detected the pseudopatients if they had been there.

Rosenhan informed the hospital that he would be sending them one or more fake patients during the next three months. The staff agreed to rate all new patients on a 10-point scale as to whether or not they were fakes. Of the 193 patients who were admitted for psychiatric treatment during this period of time, 41 were labeled fakes by at least one staff member, 23 were considered suspect by at least one psychiatrist, and 19 were labeled "suspicious" by both a psychiatrist and one other staff member. At the end of the diagnosing and evaluating, Rosenhan revealed that he had not sent any pseudopatients to that hospital.[48]

Rosenhan concludes from these two studies, " . . . any diagnostic process that lends itself so readily to massive errors of this sort cannot be a very reliable one." [49] In addition he admits, "We now know that we cannot distinguish insanity from sanity." [50] Michael Taylor and Richard Abrams evaluated 620 individuals admitted to state university hospital psychiatric units and found psychiatric misdiagnosis to be widespread. They report, "As many as four-fifths of those being diagnosed schizophrenic may not have schizophrenia at all." [51] In many ways these studies have been embarrassing and disturbing to psychotherapists, and they should cause us to question the whole system of psychotherapeutic diagnosis as well as treatment.

Not Guilty by Reason of Insanity

A number of serious problems arise with misdiagnosis, one of which has to do with our court system. In relation to criminal insanity, Rosenhan asks this question:

> How many have feigned insanity in order to avoid the criminal consequences of their behavior, and, conversely, how many would rather stand trial than live interminably in a psychiatric hospital—but are wrongly thought to be mentally ill? [52]

Our judicial system permits a plea of "not guilty by reason of insanity." The reasoning behind the plea is that a person with a deranged mind is not to be held responsible for his behavior. The burden of proof is on the defense, and the method of that proof is through psychotherapeutic diagnosis. The court recognizes the psychiatrist and the clinical psychologist as professional experts in such matters. The assumption of the court is that the professional expert can tell the sane from the insane. This assumption exists both in and out of the courtroom.

In regard to this senseless system that is letting people get away with murder, psychiatrist Abraham Halpern says, "I'm concerned for society, but I must admit I am also concerned for my profession, with psychiatry becoming a literal laughingstock from one shore to the other." [53] Jay Ziskin, who is a psychologist from a California State University, expresses this reservation about the validity of diagnosis in criminal cases:

> A psychiatric diagnosis is more likely to be wrong than right. It is even more likely to be wrong when trying to assess the mental condition at some time previous to the examination.[54]

So far we have seen that psychotherapeutic diagnosis is a disaster both in terms of poor test integrity and in misdiagnosis by professionals. If we apply these conclusions to the courts, it is frightening to think of how many false pleas of insanity have been validated by psychotherapists and how many more are yet to be. Also frightening is the weakness of a system that is trusted by the courts to tell the sane from the insane and yet fails to do so.

After studying a group of 240 men who had been declared insane by the courts, the authors of *The Criminal Personality*[55] felt that, of all these men, only about three percent were too disturbed mentally to be responsible for their actions. The rest had committed their crimes by deliberate choice. Then, when it looked as though they were going to be convicted, they feigned mental illness.

After sixteen years of study, the authors declare, "The criminal does his best to convince others of his insanity. Once he accomplishes this and is committed to a mental hospital, he tries to show others that he is no longer sick." [56] They found that a number of these men had actually studied psychology and its legal implications in order to become experts in producing just the right symptoms at the right time. In reviewing these observations in *Psychology Today,* Michael Serrill reports, "Even their severest critics do not question Yochelson and Samenow's assertion that their subjects were not mentally ill, or at least not as mentally ill as they were originally purported to be." [57]

Conclusion

Psychotherapy is a system that not only misdiagnoses in court under oath, but also in public and with impunity. There is a great deal of both misdiagnosis and mistreatment in psychotherapy. Where there should be concern, there is confidence. Nevertheless, both diagnosis and treatment are being attacked more today than ever before and by more eminent people than ever before since psychotherapy took hold of the public psyche. One group of researchers says, "Unfortunately, psychotherapists themselves have often set the stage for the 'attacks' on psychotherapy by excessive, unsubstantiated claims regarding its applicability and potency." [58]

Instead of recognizing the fallacies of psychotherapy, we have hailed it as a science and have trusted its conclusions, theories, and methods of diagnosis. Although it purports to be a science and although it attempts to align itself with the medical world and apply the medical model, it falls short of the objectivity and testability of science. Although it claims to dispense knowledge about the human condition, it has revealed few hard facts and has filled the vacuum with a collage of theories. Psychotherapy has consistently failed to discriminate between various personality disorders through diagnosis.

Furthermore, it has regularly failed to distinguish between the sane and insane. Psychotherapy is not a coherent science in principle or in theory, diagnosis, or treatment.

Part Four

14. Four Psychotherapeutic Streams

From Genesis to Revelation, running water symbolizes cleansing, healing, and life. Four pure, life-sustaining rivers flowed forth from the Garden of Eden. The water of life poured forth from the rock to sustain the children of Israel in the wilderness. Jesus offered living water to the Samaritan woman at the well. He further declared to His followers, "He that believeth on me, as the scripture hath said, out of his belly shall flow rivers of living water" (John 7:38). In the book of Revelation, the apostle John recorded his vision:

> And he shewed me a pure river of water of life, clear as crystal, proceeding out of the throne of God and of the Lamb. (Rev. 22:1)

Jesus said, "If any man thirst, let him come unto me, and drink" (John 7:37). Jesus was not speaking of literal thirst, but of spiritual thirst, for He knew that such thirst can only be satisfied with spiritual life. When Jesus gives life, He brings cleansing and healing to the soul, which includes the mind, will, and emotions.

People are at least as thirsty for life and for mental-emotional health as they have ever been. And yet, in their thirsty quest they have been led to the four polluted streams rather than to the River of Living Water. These four polluted streams represent the four major models or streams of psychotherapy. After presenting a brief description of each of the four streams, we will examine some of the forms of psychotherapy and the ideas they contain.

The first polluted stream is the psychoanalytic model, which is based on the work of Sigmund Freud. He believed that those people who were drinking from the River of Living Water were sick. He decided to devise another stream, emphasizing the mental factors of human behavior and portraying the individual as being dominated by instinctual, biological drives and by unconscious desires and motives. Basic to this view is the belief that our behavior is determined at a very early age. This idea is known as psychic determinism, which is contrary to the biblical concept of free will.

The second polluted stream is the behavioristic model, which also stresses determinism rather than free will and personal responsibility. It says that freedom of choice is only an illusion. This model rejects the introspective study of man and stresses the external and observable behavior. Rather than exploring the inner psychic phenomena as explanatory causes, it focuses on the outer behavioristic results. While the psychoanalytic model speaks of psychic determinism, the behavioristic model proposes biological, genetic, and environmental determinism. Two names associated with this model are John Watson and B. F. Skinner.

The third polluted stream of psychology gives us the humanistic model of man. It is of more recent origin and emerged as a "third force" in psychology in the 1960's under the leadership of Gordon Allport, Abraham Maslow, and Carl Rogers. Contrary to the first two streams, the humanistic model considers men to be free and self-directed rather than determined. The one unifying theme of this model is the self, which involves the self concept, individuality, the search for values, personal fulfillment, and the potential for personal growth. On the surface it sounds good, but the focus is on self rather than on God; the source for growth is self rather than the River of Living Water.

The fourth and most recent polluted stream is the existential or transpersonal model of man. This model, like the humanistic model, considers man to be a free agent who is responsible for his life. It places faith in the inner experience of the individual for dealing with his deepest problems. One of the important themes of the existential model is that of death. Themes such as what lies beyond death, the meaning of death, and the purpose and value of life are explored in this stream. Although the existential model gives us a religious view of man, it encourages the individual to break away from old patterns and to create his own values, his own religion, and his own god. Existential psychotherapists are critical of anyone who is dependent upon a religious creed or authority outside of himself.[1]

It is interesting that it has taken psychotherapy so long to "discover" the religious nature of man. Psychotherapy at its very inception considered religion to be either a weakness or flaw, on the one hand, or a myth, on the other. However, just because psychotherapy has turned to the religious nature of man, this does not mean that it is turning people back to God. Psychotherapy does not lead to the worship of the God of Abraham, Isaac, and Jacob, nor does it encourage belief in the Bible as the inspired Word of God.

We do not need the new, fourth stream, religiously oriented psychotherapists to tell us about the religious nature of man. The church has known about it all the time. And, we particularly do not need them because they have a different god and a different gospel. What we do need is to turn to the River of Living Water and learn to drink the life force freely given by our Creator and Sustainer.

From the four polluted streams flow more than 200 psychotherapeutic approaches. It is not our purpose to examine all of these systems but rather to describe representative approaches in order to give a panoramic view of the psychotherapies that are being sold for relief of mental-emotional disorders. Also, we are not attempting to place the following psychotherapies into any one stream because overlap often occurs.

We have excluded behavioristic psychotherapeutic approaches such as behavior modification because of their emphasis on the external aspects of personality. However, excluding them does not mean that we endorse them, but merely that we are limiting the scope of this book to those forms of psychotherapy that have to do with the inner psychic processes. However, we might mention in passing that one author reports, "A major recent and careful study found little outcome difference between traditional psychotherapy and behavior therapy." [2]

15. Psychoanalysis

Sigmund Freud is the most prominent name in all psychotherapy. He has developed a complex set of theories to describe the human personality and to attempt to understand and treat mental-emotional disorders. Basic to these theories is what Freud described as the unconscious portion of the mind. The unconscious part of the psyche is that which is hidden from us and not open to our direct knowledge. The usual analogy is that of an iceberg, with most of the mind submerged and hidden.

Freud believed that the unconscious portion of the mind, rather than the conscious, influences all of a person's thoughts and actions. In fact, he believed that the unconscious not only influences, but determines everything an individual does. Such psychic determinism was considered by Freud to be established within the unconscious during the first five years of life. His supposed evidence for the existence of the unconscious is found in dreams, phobias, and slips of the tongue. A phobia is an irrational fear, while a slip of the tongue is saying something that one does not consciously intend to say.

Since Freud proposed the doctrine of the unconscious and its related theories, his work has been widely accepted and admired and has significantly influenced the writing and thinking of this century. Yet this constellation of theories about the human psyche is actually only a set of one man's fantasies. These theories have been elevated from fantasy to fact, accepted as gospel truth, and applied to almost every area of human endeavor. Let us remember that we are dealing with unproven opinions, not facts; with ideas, not reality.

Freud invented psychoanalysis as a method for treating mental-emotional disorders and particularly for investigating the unconscious portion of the mind. Psychoanalysis has influenced most of contemporary psychotherapy and is one of its most sacred systems. It is only one of the many brand names, but it is considered the Cadillac of cures and is known as the fountainhead of Western psychotherapy.

The method of psychoanalysis supposedly exposes the unconscious through the process of free association and dream analysis. In free association, which is the central activity in psychoanalysis, the patient reveals both his thought life and his dreams. Through this ritual of unrestrained verbalization and dream description, the individual is theoretically unveiling his unconscious to the analyst, who in turn supposedly gains deep understanding into the patient's psyche.

People continually demonstrate both their confidence and ignorance concerning the subjectivity of psychoanalysis and other forms of psychotherapy by asking therapists the meaning of their dreams. The honest answer to any question having to do with what a dream means is that no one really knows. In the Bible Joseph confessed that he could not interpret dreams, but that only God could explain the meaning of a dream. Just because Freud and numerous others have offered interpretations of dreams, it does not mean that there is any validity to this practice.

At the present time we neither know what dreams mean nor how they originate. Dream theories range from causation by instinctual drives to mere electrochemical activity.[3] The unfortunate deception is that analysts often give their own subjective interpretations of the dreams as though they are objective truth. And through this process another layer of subjectivity is added to psychotherapy and many people are further duped into believing what is not true.

As with nearly all psychotherapeutic concepts, the interpretation of free association is pure unadulterated, unproven opinion. It is actually the loosest kind of theory based upon invented symbols and vague inferences. It is a fuzzy, hazy, soft collection of ideas which has never been proven but is propagated as truth. It is a hunting expedition into the unknown.

To demonstrate this and to show the pollution in the psycho-analytic stream of thought, let us examine some of Freud's basic theories.

The cornerstone of the psychoanalytic process is an array of theories that revolve around the unconscious. Contained within the theory of the unconscious is the theory of infantile sexuality and contained within the maze of the theory of infantile sexuality is the theory of the Oedipus complex. Therefore, in order to understand what psychoanalysis is really all about, one must at least have a glimpse into the theory of infantile sexuality and, in particular, the Oedipus complex. Our purpose in describing these theories is not to surprise or shock, but to reveal the burlesque formulations upon which psychoanalysis proudly stands.

The theory of infantile sexuality has captivated the minds of many and easily tantalizes the imagination. The Oedipus complex, the theory within a theory, is a real tour de force of subjective, distorted and dishonest reasoning presented as truth. It involves feelings of lust, homicide, and incest.

According to the theory of infantile sexuality, the first few years of life pretty much determine all that follow. Freud believed that during the first five or six years of life each human being throughout the entire world and since the beginning of mankind is confronted with certain stages of development. Failure to successfully pass through these stages or experiencing a trauma during one of these stages supposedly results in inexplicable damage to one's psyche. Freud identified the four stages as the oral, the anal, the phallic, and the genital.

In normal development, the four stages of infantile sexuality follow one another and occur at certain ages. The oral stage runs from birth to eighteen months; the anal stage from eighteen months to three years; the phallic stage from three to five or six years; and the genital stage runs through puberty. All four stages have to do with sexuality, and Freud has related adult characteristics and mental-emotional disorders to childhood experiences within the various stages. The first three stages will be presented here and particularly the phallic stage with its Oedipus complex.

During the oral stage of development everything centers

around the mouth and its activities, which are primarily sucking, biting, chewing, and spitting out. Freud related all of this to sexuality and compared sucking to sexual intercourse. He also considered such infantile activities as thumb or toe sucking to be early forms of childhood masturbation.

During the anal stage, the center of attention shifts to the lower end of the intestinal tract. Here again the main activity, which is defecation, is related to sexuality. Just as there was pleasure associated with sucking and chewing, there is pleasure in the act of expelling waste. And this act, according to Freud, is related to sexual pleasure.

The third stage of development is called the phallic stage, and the center of attention is the genital organs. It is in this stage that we see the dark, muddy water of the Freudian psychoanalytic stream. Within this stage of development, Freud identified what he called the Oedipus complex. He considered it to be one of his greatest discoveries because of its supposed universal application to man. He said, "Every new arrival on this planet is faced by the task of mastering the Oedipus complex; anyone who fails to do so falls a victim to neurosis." [4]

Since the Oedipus complex is Freud's interpretation of the Greek play entitled *Oedipus Rex* by Sophocles, let us examine this legend and see what Freud did with it. The play opens with a large crowd of people seeking aid from Oedipus, King of Thebes, because a mysterious pestilence has swept the land. Oedipus informs the crowd that he has sent Creon to seek counsel from the oracle at Delphi. Creon returns with word that the pestilence will abate when the murderer of Laius, the former King of Thebes, has been found and banished.

As the tale unfolds, we learn that many years earlier the oracle of Delphi had prophesied that any son born to King Laius of Thebes would murder him. In response to the prophecy, Laius had taken his infant son, pierced his feet with a nail, and left him on a mountain to die. The child, however, did not die but was found by a shepherd who named him Oedipus. The shepherd then brought Oedipus to the childless King and Queen of Corinth, who then raised Oedipus as their own son.

When Oedipus became a young man, he happened to seek

information from the oracle at Delphi, who predicted that he would kill his own father and marry his mother. Because he loved the only parents that he knew, he decided not to return home lest he commit such loathsome acts. Instead, he turned and went the other way. As he traveled along the narrow mountainous roadway, a chariot met him going the opposite direction. Since the two could not pass one another, the rider in the chariot harshly ordered Oedipus aside. Oedipus stepped aside, but when the chariot's wheels smashed into his foot, he reacted by killing the charioteer and the rider. Although Oedipus did not recognize him, the rider was his own true father Laius.

Then, after arriving in Thebes, Oedipus solved the riddle of the Sphinx and was rewarded with the hand of the recently widowed Queen Jocasta. Not realizing that she was his mother, Oedipus married her. When the story comes to a close and the truth of the relationship is known, Jocasta hangs herself and Oedipus pierces his own eyes with a pin from her garment and goes blind into banishment.

The story is a classic tragedy in the sense that the main character brings about his own destruction. However, unlike Freud's analysis, Oedipus loved and honored the parents who raised him. Although he did indeed murder his natural father and marry his own mother, he did so without knowing that he was their son. Freud distorted this well-known legend to demonstrate an incredible idea that is more a testimony to his own imagination than a universal truth about mankind. We will now see how Freud transformed *Oedipus Rex* into the Oedipus complex and how he twisted a legend into a supposed reality.

Freud distorted this legend by stating that during the phallic stage of development every boy desires to kill his father and have sexual intercourse with his mother, and every girl has a desire to kill her mother and to have sexual intercourse with her father. Freud attributed these desires to all children between the ages of three and six. According to this theory, both the boy and girl love the mother at the beginning and resent the father because he is a rival for the mother's attention. This idea persists in the boy until he finally, unconsciously desires the death or absence of his father, whom he considers his rival, and wants to have sexual intercourse with his mother.

The system is different for girls, however. Freud said that during a girl's early development she discovers that the boy has a protruding sex organ while she has only a cavity. According to Freud's theory, the girl holds her mother responsible for her condition, which causes hostility. She thus transfers her love from her mother to her father because he has the valued organ, which she wants to share with him in sex.

The madness is not yet complete, for Freud describes how this hostility and sensuousness are resolved. In Freud's murky and mad story, filled with fantasy and fabrication, the boy resolves the Oedipus complex through fear of castration. The boy, according to Freud, unconsciously fears that his father will cut off his penis as a punishment for his sexual desire for his mother. This fear successfully brings the boy through this stage of development by causing him to give up or retreat from his unconscious lustful desires.

The girl, on the other hand, fears that her mother will injure her genital organ because of her sexual desire directed at her father. But, within Freud's wild scheme the girl senses that she has already been castrated and thus ends up desiring the male sex organ. The female castration anxiety results in what Freud called "penis envy." According to Freud, every woman is merely a mutilated male who resolves her castration anxiety by wishing for the male sex organ.

To further compound Freud's bizarre beliefs, some analysts apply here a concept called "fellatio" from the oral stage of development. Fellatio, a most hallowed analytic concept, literally means "to suck." According to those analysts, a female may so desperately desire the male sex organ that she wants to take possession of it with her mouth. According to this theory, a woman can, because of her so-called mutilated condition, unconsciously desire to take the valued organ into her mouth to compensate for the penis she wishes she had. There is no complementary statement made about the male in the phallic stage of development. The lopsideness and extreme chauvinism of Freud's theory is further distorted by those analysts who combine fellatio with penis envy. The concept of fellatio may be the very prism through which a psychiatrist may analyze an unsuspecting female patient.

Do you see how Freud established a system of genital superiority for men and genital inferiority for women? Not only does he designate sexual superiority to the male, but he describes the female as mutilated, with a cavity rather than a powerful protruding organ. Do you see what Freud did with half of mankind? The therapy itself emphasizes a kind of bizarre sexuality that could only have originated in the mind of a male chauvinist. Needless to say, Freud's view of mankind does not fit the creation story in which "God created man in his own image, in the image of God created he him; male and female created he them. . . . And God saw every thing that he had made, and, behold, it was very good" (Gen. 1:27, 31).

Freud went on to postulate that if the Oedipus complex is properly resolved the like-sex parent becomes a model for the child. However, if it remains unresolved, it can continue to influence subsequent behavior through the unconscious portion of the mind. This myth, raised to the level of reality, is supposed to explain certain mental-emotional disorders. Infantile sexuality with its Oedipus complex is the divining rod of the psychoanalyst. His hunting expedition into the psychic past is viewed through the lens of infantile sexuality.

In exploring the tabernacle of psychoanalysis, we have come from the outer court of the unconscious to the inner court of infantile sexuality, and finally into the psychoanalytic holy of holies, the Oedipus complex. As Freud's theories are unveiled, we see lust, incest, castration anxiety, and, for a woman, penis envy. And Freud was convinced that all of these are psychologically determined by age five or six. Can you think of a more macabre, twisted and even demonic explanation for human sexuality and mental disorders than Freud's central theory of infantile sexuality? Thomas Szasz's response is this: "By dint of his rhetorical skill and persistence, Freud managed to transform an Athenian myth into an Austrian madness." He calls this "Freud's transformation of the saga of Oedipus from legend to lunacy." [5]

Through the element of Greek drama, Freud has convinced

the world that every child is filled with a desire for incest and homicide, every child desires sexual intercourse with the parent of the opposite sex, every child unconsciously wants the like-sex parent to die, and every child is confronted with castration anxiety. He has so successfully perpetrated his deceit on mankind that otherwise intelligent people not only believe the myth to be reality itself, but actually engage in its madness either as therapists or as patients. People continue to flock to the psychoanalytic couch as lambs to the slaughter, many of them ignorant of what lies in store for them. And we keep on hearing how this country needs more people trained in this mania in order to help us back to mental-emotional health.[6]

The elevation of this legend from myth to truth should have been rejected forever at its outset. But instead, Freud's peculiar interpretation and universal application were eagerly received as truth and hailed as the psychological source of salvation for troubled souls. The fallen mind that "strains at a gnat and swallows a camel" opened wide and believed a lie. This mind that could not exercise enough faith to believe in a personal God and a personal Saviour took a giant leap of faith and wholeheartedly received the Freudian gospel of salvation. Not able to accept the "faith once delivered unto the saints," the fallen mind canonized Sigmund Freud, believed and proclaimed his impossible dream, and worshipped a goulish nightmare!

Contemporary man rejected the biblical concept of universal sin, but accepted the doctrine of universal childhood fantasies of incest and homicide. He denied the very thought of the fallen nature of man as described in Scripture, but believed in a powerful unconscious, which is motivated by infantile sexuality. He trusted those who preached that the Oedipus complex, castration anxiety, and penis envy (for women) psychically determine the entire life of every individual.

Once more we need to remember that Freud's panorama of ideas is just theory. Let us not confuse theory and fact. Let us not confuse reality with one man's perverted explanation of it. Although there is a portion of our minds to which we do not seem to have direct access, it does not follow that Freud's theory about the unconscious is true. And while there is truth in the idea that all infants begin with an intimate relationship to their mothers and that children model themselves after their like-sex parent, it does not follow that Freud's explanations are true. O. Hobart Mowrer warns us of "the internal weakness of psychoanalysis, both as formal structure and as a system of practice." [7]

Because Freud's theory depends upon the unknown, invisible unconscious, there is no way to either prove or disprove the theory. However, we can say that there is presently more criticism and less confidence in Freud's theories than ever before. In fact, Mowrer also states in his book *The Crisis in Psychiatry and Religion*, "Today we can say, without fear of contradiction, that psychoanalysis has *not* been a 'success,' in this or any other country." [8] (Italics his.) E. Fuller Torrey in his book *The Death of Psychiatry* says, "Psychiatry is dying now because it has finally come to full bloom and, as such, is found not to be viable." [9]

A number of explanations of how and why Freud came up with such unusual theories as those of infantile sexuality and the Oedipus complex have been suggested. Many believe them to be the result of Freud's own distorted childhood and his own mental-emotional disturbances. In a letter to a friend, dated October 15, 1897, Freud confessed his own emotional involvement with his mother and nursemaid in a series of flowing memories and dreams.[10] Then he announced, "I have found, in my own case too, falling in love with the mother and jealousy of the father, and I now regard it as a universal event of early childhood." [11] Freud referred to his own Oedipus complex as a condition of neurosis, "my own hysteria." [12]

Freud's theory, then, is a projection of his own sexual aberrations upon all mankind. He chose to share his neurosis with the world as a universal psychological absolute. Carl Jung, one of Freud's closest early associates, reported that Freud once said to him, "My dear Jung, promise me never to abandon the sexual theory, that is the most essential thing of all. You see, we must make a dogma of it, an unshakable bulwark." [13] Mowrer describes Freud as "the Pied Piper who beguiled us into serious misconceptions and practices." [14] He has titillated the minds, tantalized the hearts and foisted a fallacy upon Western man. This is the man who calls those who believe in God "sick" and then offers instead a sick view of mankind, based upon a distorted myth and a theory about a part of the mind that no one has ever seen.

Psychic Determinism

Contained within the theory of the unconscious is not only the theory of infantile sexuality but also the theory of psychic determinism. According to this theory we are what we are because of the effect of the unconscious upon our entire life. Freud believed that "we are 'lived' by unknown and uncontrollable forces." [15] These forces, according to Freud, are in the unconscious and control us in the sense that they influence all that we do. Thus, we are puppets of the unknown and unseen unconscious, shaped by these forces during our first six years of existence. As we pass from one psychosexual stage of development to another, our psyches are shaped by people in our environment and especially by our parents.

Psychic determinism establishes a process of blame that begins in the unconscious and ends with the parent. Freud removes a person's responsibility for his behavior by teaching that everyone has been predetermined by his unconscious, which has been shaped by the treatment given him by his parents during the first few years of life. The result of this parental treatment, according to Freud, may be abnormal behavior, which he described by such ugly words as *oral fixation, sadistic, obsessive-compulsive*, and *unresolved Oedipus complex.*

The meaning of these psychoterms is not important because they are all theories. They are merely punitive labels that are used to condemn and destroy certain individuals. Moreover, these psychoterms deny the responsibility of the individual and pigeon hole him into an almost no-exit prison for which the psychoanalyst holds the only supposed key. If psychic damage occurs, the only escape is through the ritual of the "wizard of id," the psychoanalyst, who is the great high priest and has access to the mysteries of the psychoanalytic holy of holies, which contains the Oedipus complex. In order to be saved from inner turmoil, desperate souls seek this shaman of symbols, rhetoric, and metaphor.

Each theory within the psychoanalytic framework is based upon merely another theory until one finds himself in a complex labyrinth with the theories of castration anxiety and penis envy within the Oedipus theory within the infantile sexuality theory within the unconscious theory, with the theory of psychic determinism pervading the stagnant water.

The theories within theories related to theories were the threads with which Freud, the master weaver, wove the web of deception so intricately that we are trapped within it. We are confused by the words and bewildered by the language. We simply do not know how to either verify or refute such a system of subjectivity that confuses and condemns us without proof. It is akin to shoveling smoke.

The whole scheme of the unconscious is a fantasy within a fantasy and a lie within a lie. It is an *Alice in Wonderland* game in which one can give words whatever meanings one chooses.

> "When *I* use a word," Humpty Dumpty said, in a rather scornful tone, "it means just what I choose it to mean—neither more nor less."
> "The question is," said Alice, "whether you *can* make words mean so many different things."
> "The question is," said Humpty Dumpty, "which is to be master—that's all." [16]

The Bible says in Proverbs 22:6, "Train up a child in the way he should go and, when he is old, he will not depart from it." The Bible strongly supports the *influence* of early training. However, there is a giant difference between being influenced and being determined. We are not stuck with our early upbringing if it happened to be bad, nor can we guarantee that someone with good upbringing will turn out well. However, we have been convinced by the Freudian fallacies that certain kinds of early training fix abnormal behavior in the adult. Thus, if an adult is poorly adjusted we conclude that he must have had poor early parenting. [17]

Victor and Mildred Goertzel investigated this fallacy. In

their book *Cradles of Eminence* they report on the early environments of over four hundred eminent men and women of the twentieth century who had experienced a wide variety of trials and tribulations during their childhood.[18] It is surprising and even shocking to discover the environmental handicaps that have been overcome by individuals who should have been psychically determined failures according to Freudian formulas. Instead of being harmed by unfortunate early circumstances, they became outstanding in many different fields of endeavor and contributed much to mankind. What might have been environmental curses seemed to act, rather, as catalysts to spawn genius and creativity. This study is not an argument for poor upbringing; it is an argument against psychic determinism.

A person need not be trapped in negative patterns of behavior established in the early years of life, for the Bible offers a new way of life. Put off the old man; put on the new. Jesus said to Nicodemus, "Ye must be born again," and He said elsewhere that new wine could not be put into old wineskins. Jesus offers new life and new beginnings. One who is born again has the spiritual capacity to overcome old ways and develop new ones through the action of the Holy Spirit, the fruit of the Spirit, and the sanctification of the believer. One wonders why so many have given up the hope of Christianity for the hopelessness of psychic determinism.

The psychoanalytic idea of determinism is absolutely contrary to the biblical doctrine of free will. From Freudian determinism it follows that one is not responsible for his behavior. After all, if his behavior has already been determined by the age of six by the unseen forces in his unconscious, how can he possibly be responsible for what he does?

The Bible teaches that man does have a free will and that he is responsible for his actions. If this were not true, why would God give us commands to follow? It would be foolish to give commands to people who are already programmed to respond in predetermined ways. Furthermore, if man were not responsible for his actions, why would God institute a system of punishment for various transgressions in the Old Testament? If a person is not responsible, then he cannot be held liable and, therefore, should not be punished. Finally, if man is not responsible for what he does, what is forgiveness all about?

Psychic determinism with its accompanying freedom from responsibility is contrary to the Word of God. We *do* have free will and God does hold us responsible for what we do. Psychic determinism has led to moral bankruptcy which in turn has led to or complicated mental failures. Man has a free will. He is able to choose to follow God's laws and to benefit intellectually and emotionally from doing so. Our God-given free will has not been replaced by unconscious determinism.

Psychic determinism supports the natural tendency in the human heart to blame circumstances or other people for our actions. This pattern emerged in the Garden of Eden when Adam blamed Eve and Eve blamed the serpent. In supporting the natural tendency to place blame elsewhere, psychoanalysis provides extensive explanations and rationale for aberrant behavior. The truth is that those who say they have no free will are lying, fooling themselves, or have truly capitulated to the fallacies of psychoanalysis. In denying the responsibility involved in free will, a person can do what he pleases; that is, he can exercise his free will under the guise of psychic determinism.

An extensive study of the criminal personality asserts that criminals commit crimes by deliberate choice.[19] This contradicts the idea of psychic determinism and the usual so-called insights of modern psychotherapy that tend to blame the environment and remove the responsibility from the individual. Part of the outcry against the criminal personality study occurred because those who conducted and reported the study placed the blame for wrong behavior back on the criminal himself. An example of this kind of response is that of Simon Dinitz, an Ohio State sociologist. He says, "They're placing the blame back on the individual and his screwed-up thinking. And they can't even give you a good explanation for why his thinking is so screwed up." [20] Responsibility for one's behavior, criminal or otherwise, is not a popular idea in many psychological and sociological circles.

On the other hand, there are some who believe that the individual may even be responsible for his own insanity in that he chooses insanity as a way of behavior. Jung referred to certain mental disorders as playacting or malingering.[21] William Glasser describes a procedure used by G. L. Harrington, a former teacher of his. According to Glasser, Harrington says:

> Hospitals are for crazy people. Everybody that is crazy has decided at some time to become crazy, has decided how he is going to act when he is crazy and, when he decides not to be crazy, he will not be crazy. He will make a conscious decision the same as you decide whether to take tea or coffee for dinner. . . .[22]

Thus, there are some who believe in individual responsibility to the extent of a person being accountable for choosing his own insanity.

Morality

Freud's view of morality is that psychological disorders occur because of society's interference with the instinctual biological needs of the individual. Freud said, ". . . we have found it impossible to give our support to conventional morality [which] demands more sacrifices than it is worth." [23] Freud felt that mental-emotional disorders were caused by the individual being too hard on himself and even encouraged people to free themselves of inhibitions in order to gratify their instincts. Freud's position was that the person's moral standards are too high and that his performance has been too good. Thus, he attempted to neutralize the person's conscience.

As a result, Freud's moral stance was one of permissiveness with respect to individual action and restraint. In particular, he felt that free fornication would be great preventive medicine and psychoprophylactic for the mind. In fact, he believed in a strong, direct relationship between a person's sex life and mental-emotional disorders. He said, ". . . factors arising in sexual life represent the nearest and practically the most momentous causes of every single case of nervous illness." [24]

However, Freud warned against giving up masturbation for intercourse because of the possibility of contracting syphilis and gonorrhea. But then he suggested, "The only alternative would be free sexual intercourse between young males and respectable girls; but this could only be resorted to if there were innocuous preventative methods," by which he meant birth control.[25] Thus, Freud's only objections to free fornication were the possibilities of venereal disease and pregnancy. Little did he anticipate our present permissive society which has achieved his great therapeutic image of free fornication. Little did he realize the sexual revolution that followed his conjectures. Little did he know that the ensuing sexual permissiveness would become the cause of more mental-emotional disorders rather than the cure.

The biblical position on fornication is clear: it is forbidden. Biblical restrictions are not a curse, as Freud would want us to believe; they bring health and healing. If such restraints lead to mental disorders, why would the Creator have instituted them? Free fornication, not biblical restraint, leads to human chaos. We see the evidence of this in the prevailing high divorce rate and abortions, both of which take a heavy toll in mental-emotional pain and stress.

Contrary to what the Freudians would have us believe, it is not freedom in this area that leads to adjustment; it is responsibility and restraint. Acting contrary to the Word of God is not only sin; it is poor preventive mental health. Thus, fornication is psychonoxious, not psychoprophylactic. Biblical restraint leads to good mental health, and biblical principles are a balm for anxiety.

The whole failure of the Freudian morality system is permissiveness, and this permissiveness has pervaded not only Freud's thinking, but also the thinking of many who followed. It became part and parcel of public attitudes about social, political, and economic issues as well as about sex. For example, it affected and influenced much of the thinking and teaching in the area of child discipline. One professor who was influenced by Freud used to say, "Never spank a child until he is old enough to understand it and when he is old enough to understand it, never spank a child." Benjamin Spock proliferated the no-spank permissiveness in his best seller *Baby and Child Care*[26] and millions of well-meaning parents accepted this Freudian foolishness without question.

There is no doubt that Spock's no-spank position is contrary to Scripture, as we are told in Proverbs 13:24: "He that spareth his rod hateth his son, but he that loveth him chasteneth him early." Discipline is a form of love. Permissiveness, on the other hand, means either indifference or hate. Also, in Proverbs 22:15 we are told, "Foolishness is bound in the heart of a child; but the rod of correction shall drive it far from him."

When Spock realized the kind of damage that his advice in child-rearing had done, he admitted that he and other professionals had actually persuaded the public that they were the only people "who know for sure how children should be managed." [27] He further admitted:

> This is a cruel deprivation that we professionals have imposed on mothers and fathers. Of course, we did it with the best of intentions. . . . We didn't realize, until it was too late, how our know-it-all attitude was undermining the self-assurance of parents.[28]

It is good news that he has recanted his former pro-permissive doctrine. He now says, "Inability to be firm is, to my mind, the commonest problem of parents in America today." [29] He further states, " . . . parental submissiveness [to children] doesn't avoid unpleasantness; it makes it inevitable." [30]

While both extremes of permissiveness and restrictiveness can be detrimental to a child, the Bible gives us the right balance between the two. We don't need Freud or any of his followers to teach us about child discipline.

The Freudian Failure

After examining the theories developed by Sigmund Freud and the practices and attitudes that followed in his wake, can we say that Freud has given us a panacea for mental-emotional health? Do his theories comprise a solution to human problems? Is infantile sexuality really the magic wand we have been looking for? The offerings of Freud and his followers are no more than man-made substitutes for the spiritual truths which our Creator has given to mankind in His Word and through the life of His Son Jesus. After many years of involvement with psychiatry, Mowrer concludes:

> I have become increasingly convinced . . . of the basic unsoundness of Freud's major premises and have, literally, read myself back into a position which can be at least loosely identified as Judeo-Christian.[31]

Mowrer had come to realize that "there is not a shred of evidence that psychoanalyzed individuals permanently benefit from the experience."[32] In fact, he predicts the fall of the psychoanalytic kingdom: "Psychoanalysis is in a state of virtual collapse and imminent demise."[33] Thomas Szasz declares:

> The cures of regular psychiatrists were and are so worthless and frightful that anyone offering a new method based on the premise of doing away with this entire therapeutic armamentarium is bound to appear compassionate.[34]

Freud first mythologized psychotherapy, then he medicalized it, scientized it, and merchandised it. He left us a supposed universal cure for mankind. However, when we look closely, we see a system which has often been described as merely a white, middle-class, occidental miasma. Its central activity of free association is not so free after all, because the patient tells the therapist what he thinks the therapist wants to hear. Jay Haley contends, ". . . a patient's productions are always being influenced by a therapist, which is why patients in Freudian analysis have dreams with more evident sexual content."[35]

To participate in the ritual of psychoanalysis one must "free associate," give up his free will, agree to be determined by his past, blame his parents, become dependent upon the therapist, permit the therapist to take the place of both parents and God, deify sex and denigrate religion, and, above all, pay large sums of money over a long period of time, in spite of the lack of evidence that this Freudian fetish is of any value.

When someone suggests psychoanalysis, beware. And be aware of the intrusion and influence of these ideas into the numerous other brands of psychotherapy existent today, for most of them are influenced greatly by Freudian thought. The Freudian fantasies have filtered into nearly all of the psychotherapeutic world. In Dante's *Inferno* there is a sign over the entrance of hell (hades) which reads, "Abandon all hope, ye who enter here." We believe that is a safe way for Christians to view psychoanalysis.

16. Scream Therapy

Within the muddy waters of the psychoanalytic stream are numerous tributaries of Freudian theory, and among them flows the questionable therapy of the Primal Scream, created by Arthur Janov. Janov superimposed his theories upon such basic concepts as the unconscious determinants of behavior, the vast influence of the early formative years on present behavior, and the need to return to the past to uncover early traumas which are buried in the unconscious.

There is a little psychoanalytic leaven in almost every psychotherapeutic loaf, but Primal Therapy has a particularly strong Freudian flavor. However, Janov invented a novel twist to the Freudian framework. He has taken the basics and added some excitement, drama, and stimulus for violent expression. He has popularized the psychic trip into the past and claims a 95 percent cure rate for customers.[36]

Soon after Janov completed his doctorate in psychology from Claremont Graduate School in 1960, he opened his private practice. The beginnings of Primal Therapy occurred during a session with a college student whom he calls Danny Wilson. In this session Wilson told Janov about a comedian whose act consisted of wandering around the stage dressed in diapers, drinking out of a baby bottle, and calling out,

"Mommy! Daddy! Mommy! Daddy!" The comedian ended his act by passing out plastic bags, vomiting into a bag, and inviting the audience to do likewise. Because of Wilson's obvious fascination with the act, Janov suggested that he might want to cry out "Mommy" and "Daddy" just as the comedian had done. Although Wilson first refused, he finally gave in and began calling out, "Mommy! Daddy! Mommy! Daddy!" The next few minutes provided the basis for Janov's new therapeutic system.

Janov noticed that Wilson became very upset and began turning and twisting in agony, with his breathing becoming rapid and sporadic. Then Wilson screeched, "Mommy! Daddy!" His movements became more convulsive and finally he let out a piercing, deathlike scream. And with this scream, Janov launched the currently much-sought-after Primal Therapy. Janov began trying it out on other clients and developed his theory accordingly. Then, he published a description of his methodology in his book *Primal Scream* in 1970, which has exceeded 200,000 copies sold.[37]

In order to dispense his brand of therapy, Janov had to build special, soundproof facilities to protect the community from the ear-piercing screams and violent verbalizations expressed during the sessions. He soon opened the Primal Institute in Los Angeles both to conduct therapy sessions and to train therapists. He recently opened a second institute in New York, and, although he originally directed everything himself, he has turned over the major operation of his institutes to his son and his ex-wife.[38] Nevertheless, Janov still maintains his authoritative influence as the Primal pope.

Primal Therapy is currently one of the very popular forms of therapy for those who can afford the $6,600 fee. The demand is so great that many psychotherapists read Janov's book and then offer similar treatment. Janov, however, would consider them unauthorized and unqualified if they have not been certified by his institute.

The sacred words of Primal Therapy are *Primal Pain*, which are always capitalized for emphasis. It is around these words that the central doctrines of Primal Therapy revolve. According to Janov, as the child grows he has a dilemma between being himself and conforming to the expectations of his parents. During this period of development, the child accumulates Pain from the injuries of unmet needs, such as not being fed when hungry, not being changed when wet, or being ignored when needing attention. Primal Pain occurs as the result of the conflicts between self need and parental expectation. Through the process of growth as conflicts continue to occur, the accumulation of Primal Pain results in what Janov calls the "Primal Pool of Pain."

When the Pool gets deep enough, just one more incident supposedly pushes the child into neurosis. This single significant incident is labeled the "major Primal Scene." Janov contends:

> The major Primal Scene is the single most shattering event in the child's life. It is that moment of icy, cosmic loneliness, the bitterest of all epiphanies. It is the time when he begins to discover that he is not loved for what he is and will not be.[39]

It is at this point that the child finally gives up the idea of being himself in order to gain his parents' love. In the process of gaining parental approval, the child supposedly seals off his real feelings and becomes an unreal self. Janov calls this disassociation from one's feelings "neurosis."

Janov believes that the Primal Scene occurs between the ages of five and seven and is buried in the unconscious. The individual builds a network of defenses against even the awareness that the Pain is there. He develops a life-style that hides the origin of the Pain and merely releases the tension caused by the Pain, but he is not able to eliminate it.

Notice here, as with the Freudian process of blame and the voyage into the past, Janov's culprit is the parents and the solution is to be found in the past. In both theories only a return to the early years can bring healing for present anxieties. Janov not only specifies a single cause of neurosis: blocked Pain; but offers a single cure, the one and only cure in all the world for neurosis: Primal Therapy.

Janov theorizes that to be cured, the neurotic must return to his major Primal Scene where he decided to give up his real self and his real feelings in exchange for the possibility of parental love. He must experience the emotions, the events, and the expectations of others as well as the accompanying Pain in order to be cured. The experience of returning to the Primal Scene and suffering the Primal Pain is called a "Primal." Primals are a necessary part of the healing process as far as Janov is concerned.

In reading Janov's book we see an absence of joy in the Primals. They seem to be universally filled with such negative human emotions as anger, fear, loneliness, and rejection. Although Primal Therapy involves both a talking out and a feeling out, feeling is supreme. The way into and out of neurosis, according to Janov, is through feeling. He says, "Neurosis is a disease of feeling." [40]

Primal Therapy, like most contemporary therapies, promises a quickie cure. It involves three weeks of intensive individual therapy, followed by six months of weekly group sessions, and culminating in one week of intensive private therapy. After this, the patient is free to have Primals on his own. During the first three weeks of individual therapy, the patient usually has his first Primal. After that, he continues to have more Primals during post-period group sessions. The therapist does everything he can to encourage the patient to get in touch with his internal Pain. A number of props, such as baby bottles, cribs, cuddly toys, life-sized photographs of parents, and even a birth simulator made out of inner tubes, have been used during these sessions.

In group sessions there is little interchange among those present. The Primal is king and the individual experience is supreme. As you can imagine, it would seem like utter chaos and outright bedlam to stumble upon such a group. Visualize some adults sucking baby bottles, others cuddling stuffed toys, still others in adult-sized cribs, one man standing with his genitals exposed, and a woman with her breasts uncovered. Then there is the birth simulator for those who want to experience the Primals that go all the way back to the womb and the birth process. Additionally, picture thirty or forty adults on the floor, gagging, thrashing, writhing, gurgling, choking and wailing. Listen to the sobbing and screeching, "Daddy, be nice!" "Mommy, help!" "I hate you! I hate you!" "Daddy, don't hurt me anymore!" "Mommy, I'm afraid!"

And all of this is punctuated by deep rattling and high-piercing screams.

Does Primal Therapy really bring emotional stability into a person's life? Janov enthusiastically claims a 95 percent cure rate. But, it depends on whom you ask. Just as with many forms of therapy, there is much in the way of testimonials, but little verifiable research. Some of Janov's critics have accused the patients of either consciously or unconsciously faking the Primals. No doubt there is some self-hypnosis and gullibility involved. Others have warned that this type of treatment could cause psychological deterioration or permanent psychosis. Some former patients have even called it emotional brainwashing.

If one listens to the testimonials of satisfied customers, one might well be impressed with the glowing claims of emotional healing and the elimination of migraine headaches, ulcers, arthritis, menstrual cramps, and asthma. Janov states that many dramatic physical changes result from his therapy. "For example," he says, "about one-third of the moderately flat-chested women independently reported that their breasts grew." [41] Janov claims that Primal Therapy is a cure-all when he declares, "But Primal Therapy *should* be able to do away with all symptoms or the premise—that symptoms are the result of Primal Pains—is not valid." [42] (Italics his.)

Such testimonials are not backed with any kind of unbiased research. Since the Janovs rule the institute and do not allow outside research teams to conduct studies, the success or failure of Primal Therapy cannot be determined apart from the subjectivity of testimonials which range all the way from praising to damning. Without outside validation from objective research groups, we cannot know the extent of help or damage that occurs.

This sick, sick, sick psychotherapy is only one of a host of similar therapies that are attracting a large number of adults seeking to find solace for the troubled soul. It is impossible to tell how many are in Primal Therapy or any one of its "friends and relations." The Primal Institute alone has numerous applications each month in spite of the $6,600 fee.

Another therapist, Daniel Casriel, in his book *A Scream*

Away from Happiness describes his method of group scream therapy.[43] He claims that thousands of people per week engage in this form of group encounter which relies heavily on screams and verbal assertiveness. During Casriel's sessions, group members hold hands and are commanded to scream. In addition to the use of the scream technique, there is much encouragement to verbally assert oneself. For example, the leader instructs the participants to assert themselves by eyeball-to-eyeball contact, with aggressive statements such as "I'm entitled!" repeated over and over again. After a little practice, they are to assert themselves by repeatedly shouting, "I'm entitled!" punctuated by obscenities.[44] The more assertive, the better; the more ventilation of aggressive and negative feelings, the better.

Leonard Berkowitz, who has extensively studied violence and aggression, disagrees with the idea that it is desirable to let out one's aggressive feelings. Those therapists that encourage such active expressions of negative emotions are called "ventilationists." Their therapies, according to Berkowitz, stimulate and reward aggression and "heighten the likelihood of subsequent violence." [45] He declares, "The evidence dictates now that it is unintelligent to encourage persons to be aggressive, even if, with the best of intentions, we want to limit such behavior to the confines of psychotherapy." [46]

Berkowitz criticizes the rejection of the intellect in these theories as well as the popular view held by ventilationists and others that it is unhealthy to suppress our feelings. He believes that "in the long run, our social and human problems can be solved only with intelligence." [47] Regarding the popularity of such therapies, he quips, " . . . most ventilationists are located on the East and West Coasts, but particularly in California; I regard them as part of California's contribution to the American Dream, along with Hollywood and Disneyland." [48]

We don't know what therapies Christians are paying for, but desperate and naive Christians are just as likely to undergo ventilationist therapies as any other. Janov, Casriel, and others have not only capitalized on the fantasies of Freud, but also on the gullibility of the public. People who are desperate to escape the emptiness and loneliness of life are willing to believe direct or implied promises backed up by a title and an office or an institute and a board of directors. And so, fantasy follows fantasy and we come full circle back to the mirage of empty promises and testimonials, which had appeared like an oasis in the desert of despair.

17. Encounter

There are numerous contemporary psychotherapies and they tend to proliferate annually. The encounter movement encompasses many forms of group therapies and approaches, including T-groups, awareness groups, sensitivity training, and Gestalt.

There is such a diversity in encounter that it is difficult to briefly describe all approaches. The size of the groups may range from two to hundreds. The methodology ranges from being structured to having almost no format at all. Some groups are conservative and use only a controlled verbal exchange with much protection for the participant; other groups operate in almost a no-holds-barred manner. Some train individuals in business and industry, and others provide opportunities for sexual experiences. Some meet on a weekly or monthly basis; others are intensive marathons.

Generally speaking, encounter may be contrasted with psychoanalysis in the following ways. Whereas in psychoanalysis the emphasis is on the past, the unconscious, and the mind; encounter glorifies the present, the conscious awareness, and the body. Direct experience is more important in encounter than indirect or intellectual experiences or insight. Whereas psychoanalysis involves a long-term relationship between the therapist and the patient, encounter is a group situation with a variety of short- or long-term interactions. In contrast to psychoanalysis, most people who participate in encounter are not suffering from extreme emotional disorders. Their problems are usually marital, occupational, or personal adjustment. Others are just bored, lonely, or looking for a new and novel experience.

With respect to morality, encounter sets few limits on acting out, loving out, and living out. One can live, love, and act in an encounter group with few restrictions. Arthur Burton reports:

> Many clients tell me that they go to encounter group centers not only for the encounter itself but for the vast opportunities for sexual experience which are to be found there. One famous encounter center offers baths in which mixed nude bathing is the rule after the sessions themselves.[49]

The actions of encounter are based on "If it feels good, do it!" Encounter encourages both experimental and exploratory actions and relationships. Participants have opportunities to experiment with a variety of partners in both conversation and intimacy and to explore previously untried actions and responses.

One of the basic assumptions of most encounter groups is that it is emotionally beneficial to be totally transparent and open. Self-exposure has become almost a therapeutic absolute in the encounter movement and influences all that is said and done. Thus, the vocabulary is usually wide open, and the use of four-letter words is encouraged and serves as a mark of achievement. Even older women, who previously may have never heard some of the expressions nor known the experiences associated with the words, participate in this verbage. This verbal badge of encounter is often displayed so that all can hear, for one cannot truly feel "in" unless he expresses himself with such encounter language.

If a person in an encounter group is opposed to or resistant to acting out and speaking out, he is encouraged by the group "to go all the way." If he resists too much he is rejected as uptight, unreal, rigid, phony, and plastic. These words along with a number of other adjectives are used to persuade the person that his reasoning is fallacious and his reluctance is unnecessary. After all, everyone is doing it; why not you? Besides, it's good for you—or so they would like you to believe.

One of the extreme forms of encounter is the marathon, during which a highly intensive experience lasts for many hours at a time over a period of two or three days. The theory behind the marathon is that, as the experience continues hour after hour, the emotions and normal defense system wear down until only the real person remains to be dealt with. We can hardly see how a tired, emotionally depleted and physically exhausted body represents the real person, but that is the theory behind this intensive form of madness.

Contrary to the confidence that people have in marathon encounters, research has never shown that either this theory or therapy has any validity in fact. Claims that the short-term intensive marathon brings long-term changes in the individual have simply never been proven. Additionally, many psychologists have indicated that lowering the normal psychological defense system may result in psychotic breakdowns or even suicide. Psychiatrist Arthur Burton refers to the marathon as "a hysterical form of encounter." [50]

The most bizarre form of encounter is the nude encounter. The late Abraham Maslow, a well-known humanistic psychologist, believed that with nudity in groups, "people would go away more spontaneous, less guarded, less defensive, not only about the shape of their behinds, but freer and more innocent about their minds as well." [51]

Paul Bindrim, the originator of the nude marathon group therapy, believes it is a real breakthrough in approaches to human improvement. One of his own therapeutic inventions to relieve the troubled mind is called "crotch eyeballing." This sounds, and is, suspiciously Freudian. It's the phallic stage of development with a new twist. The crotch, he contends, is the focus of many hang-ups. This technique involves one nude member lying on his/her back with legs spread apart and the rest of the group staring at his/her exposed genital-anal area for an extended period of time. Such activity is supposed to be a refreshing boost to each person involved, a real salve for the anxious soul. Of course no research supports such wild assertions.

Both the extreme and the less extreme forms of encounter have made their mark on our society and continue to influence the thoughts and actions of many people. Daniel Casriel predicts, "It is my conviction that organized group interaction will soon explode into a force of massive significance in the United States." [52] Carl Rogers believes that "the whole movement toward intensive group experience in all its forms has profound significance, for both today and tomorrow." [53] He calls this intensive group experience "one of the most exciting developments of our time." [54] Considering the vast influence of the encounter movement, we need to look objectively at the results. Does this movement have positive or negative effects on individuals? Is it a valid and useful method for helping people?

The claims for cure and relief in encounter are widespread, but does it really work? In a book entitled *Encounter Groups: First Facts*, the authors report on an extensive study conducted with Stanford University students. Since entrance requirements at Stanford are high and the students are bright, one would expect the chances for therapeutic success to be much higher than for the average population. These participants also had high expectations for improvement.[55]

The authors of the study selected mostly psychiatrists and psychologists as leaders. "All were highly experienced group leaders, and were uniformly esteemed by their colleagues as representing the best of their approach." [56] Thus, the select group of participants and the specially chosen leaders should have demonstrated positive results as to the effectiveness of encounter.

Seventeen separate encounter groups were formed for the study and represented ten different theoretical approaches. Students were assigned to the groups in a random fashion. In addition, a control group of students who received no treatment was set up. Research was conducted on all participants and on the control group several weeks before the encounter groups began, then again shortly after the encounter experience, and then finally six to eight months later.

After six months every participant and control were asked to describe changes he had noticed in his own outlook and behavior. According to the authors, there was no significant difference between the students who had received the encounter experience and those who had not. Relatives and friends close to each participant and control were also asked to describe behavior changes in the students. Those close to the encounter participants rated 80 percent of them as having made some positive change. However, those close to the control group rated 83 percent as having improved. Again, there is no significant difference between the two groups, but what a revelation!

Shortly after the encounter experience 65 percent of the encounter group reported some positive change and most of them believed that the change would last. A ratio was established between those who rated the experience high and those who rated it poor. The ratio shortly after the experience was 4.7 to 1. However, in spite of the fact that most expected the change to be lasting, after six months the ratio declined to 2.3 to 1.[57] Obviously the enthusiasm about the benefits of encounter had diminished.

The most disturbing result of the study was the casualty rate for the encounter participants. The authors state:

> We put persons in this category only if we found evidence of serious psychological harm six to eight months after the group ended and if we felt that their psychological difficulties could reasonably be attributed to the group experience.[58]

The casualty rate, which excludes those who exhibited negative change, was 9 percent. Considering the select group of students and leaders involved, the desire of the leaders to be successful because of the comparisons to be made, and the conservative definition used for casualty, 9 percent seems enormously high. The authors of the study conclude, "It appears that encounter groups are less effective than individual psychotherapy in changing individuals and somewhat more likely to cause damage." [59]

Psychic casualties, including mental breakdowns, divorces, and even suicides as a result of encounter, are known about but little publicized. Jerome Frank warns, "Thus, such groups can easily become exercises in mutual exploitation and can seriously damage some participants." [60] It seems that, with the results of the extensive research now being conducted in the area of encounter, some consumer protection is in order. When we combine the potential danger of the encounter with the small possibility of success, one wonders why people spend valuable time and pay money for it.

With the possibility of casualties and psychological damage to participants, one would hope that the encounter leaders could spot possible casualties and advise them not to participate. However, another disturbing discovery of the study just reported was that the group leaders were the least able to identify the ones who became casualties. The judgments of both the group leaders and the group members were evaluated. The conclusion was that the leader's judgments about casualties in his own group were not as reliable as those of the coparticipants. The authors state:

> The coparticipants' perceptions of who got hurt were much more reliable; in fact, they were more accurate than any other single criterion.[61]

Encounter is a synthetic and artificial experience. The hope is that a person will change in this special setting and then walk out into life a better worker, a better spouse, a better parent, a better person. However, aside from testimonials, the research simply does not support such a notion. Rodney Luther says:

> We are concerned that 25 to 40 percent of persons sent to sensitivity gain nothing and very possibly lose some highly valuable behavioral assets. Even in actual war, win-loss ratios of this order of magnitude are impossible to justify.[62]

Unfortunately the leaders in the encounter movement have overemphasized successes based upon testimonials and ignored failures. Those who have been pushed into mental-emotional disorders or even suicide are overlooked as casually as one might look at the body count of a war that occurred over 500 years ago. As the late Fritz Perls said:

> So, if you want to go crazy, commit suicide, improve, get "turned on," or get an experience that will change your life, that's up to you. . . . You came here out of your own free will. [63]

This is a leader's way of saying if something happens to the participant, it is not the leader's fault; that is, unless it's good and then he might take the credit. Sigmund Koch says in an article, "The Image of Man in Encounter Groups,"

> . . . the group movement is the most extreme excursion thus far of man's talent for reducing, distorting, evading and vulgarizing his own reality.[64]

In spite of the questionable morality of encounter ("If it

feels good, do it.'') and in spite of negative results in people's lives and even casualties, the encounter business has moved into the realm of Christendom. Without examining the broad spectrum of sensitivity training and encounter, the church has in many areas adopted encounter group techniques and has invited the encounter movement right into its own social structure. Arthur Burton says of the encounter movement:

> I am in all seriousness when I say that it may soon represent the Judeo-Christian emphasis on individualization applied to vast numbers of people who can no longer be formally Christian but who want to be fully human. The professionally religious have sensed this ahead of some of the rest of us and this may explain their deep participation in encounter work.[65]

This is a sad state of affairs. The encounter movement not only has a morality that is not biblical, but it is a false substitute for the saving reality of the Bible and Christianity. This moving away from the mind to the senses, from reason to emotions, and from the spirit to the body, this glorification of self-disclosure and deification of direct experience have never proven to be an antidote for human ills. Anyone who leaves the Living Waters to drink out of the broken cisterns of encounter is like Esau who exchanged his birthright for a pot of beans.

18. Est

In recent years the market has been flooded with a great number of pop psychotherapies. A recent madness from this new surge of psychological pottage is one that has grown by such leaps and bounds that it merits our attention. It is a combination of psychological and philosophical thought all wrapped up into a psychotherapeutic system that denies being psychotherapy. However, it promises like, acts like, and sells like any other psychotherapy in the marketplace, only more so.

The lack of official designation as psychotherapy is only a necessary protection for its founder who has no license or training to practice in the field. Nevertheless, the state of Hawaii says that it is a form of psychotherapy and therefore requires the presence of a licensed psychologist or M.D. to supervise each session.[66]

The name of this conglomeration of Eastern thought and Western psychotherapy is est, which stands for Erhard Seminar Training. Est was developed and is dispensed by Jack Rosenberg, who adopted the pseudonym of Werner Hans Erhard after he abandoned his wife and four children. Previous to his invention of est, Erhard had various jobs in car, magazine, and encyclopedia sales. Along the way he was involved in Scientology and was an instructor in Mind Dynamics, which, incidentally, went out of business and was sued by the State of California for false claims and for practicing medicine without a license.

During his sales career, Erhard demonstrated a great ability to organize, train, and motivate sales people. He now uses this exceptional talent in the packaging and commercialization of est. His organizational and psychosales abilities have created a California cult, now gone nationwide, of multimillion dollar proportions. After the enthusiastic est converts receive promotional training in Erhard's graduate seminars, they comprise his gigantic unpaid sales force.

This system of supposed self-transformation is dispensed in a sixty-hour course, which meets over two consecutive weekends and sells for $300. Since there is little personal interaction between the trainers and the trainees, they train 250 to 300 people at a crack. At the present time over 160,000 individuals have taken the course, and it is estimated that an additional 3,000 people take the training each month.

Est seems to rely more on method than on content. The content is not the message, "the medium is the message," and the medium is a strong-armed method used to coerce the unsuspecting subject into a new belief system. The method is so powerful that the poor, gullible trainee is bludgeoned into believing whatever brand of instant regeneration Erhard and his militaristic assistants might dispense.

Nevertheless, the content is important to the extent that it places most est graduates into a new philosophical and moral position. At first blush est is a system that fits in with what the middle class values and wants. There is an emphasis on accepting oneself, since each trainee learns he is perfect just the way he is. Additionally, the element of individual responsibility makes it sound almost Christian.

Along with these positive possibilities, the content is a hodge podge of Freud, Jung, Transactional Analysis, Gestalt, common sense psychology, and Eastern philosophy, sugarcoated to sell in the middle-class market. It has been packaged with the consumer in mind, the same as everything else that Erhard sold during his careers.

One basic assumption of est is the anti-biblical message that the world has no meaning or purpose. Because of this assumption, much time is spent on tearing down one's belief system. The trainees learn that their beliefs are not only unimportant; they are obstacles to growth. If they venture to try to support a belief, they are ridiculed and made to look stupid in front of the entire assembly. "Belief," says Erhard, "is a disease." [67] It is not belief but rather experience that is supreme. According to Erhard:

> The truth believed is a lie. If you go around preaching the truth, you are lying. The truth can only be experienced. . . .
>
> The horrible part about it is that the truth is so damn believable, people usually believe it instead of experiencing it. [68]

According to *Newsweek*, "The purpose of est is to make each trainee experience the 'satisfaction' of becoming the author of his own subjective universe of sensations, emotions and ideas." [69] This experience is the *sine qua non* of est called "getting it." It is the peak experience of this psychopottage. When you "get it" you have arrived. You are now a part of a special elite group. According to est, anyone who has not "gotten it" can't knock "it," because they haven't experienced "it" themselves.

The so-called purpose of est is for people to "get it," but how does one know when he's got it? Mark Brewer, a journalist who investigated est, reported his experience in *Psychology Today*. He says, "When you know you're a mechanical anus, you've 'got it.' " [70] That is what thousands of people are paying for and believing.

To perpetuate and expand his system, Erhard has a

smooth method of word-of-mouth advertising. At the end of the sessions, the graduates are encouraged to get others to take the training. However, they are cautioned not to discuss the content or method of the training with the new potential customers, since foreknowledge might prevent people from "getting it." Another reason is that the training cannot be explained; it can only be experienced. Therefore, when the new trainees arrive they do not know what they are really getting into.

And, what they are getting into is a fiendishly devised system that is calculated to convert large numbers and to convince them to recruit others to their new-found faith. Erhard has been enormously successful at this game and has captured the hearts and minds of those in the middle and upper middle classes. Advocates of est include prominent doctors, lawyers, university professors, movie actors, and even corporation executives.

Now let us look at the malevolent method of est. It all begins with about 250 to 300 people at a swank hotel. The size of the group should not be overlooked, since large numbers lend an atmosphere conducive to the use of mob psychology. The group is seated and the training begins. Enrollees are instructed in the house rules for the seminar: no talking unless called upon, no smoking, eating, taking notes, moving around, or leaving the room, even to go to the bathroom. This deprivation is the beginning of the method of transformation from ignorance to "getting it" and from doubt to zombie-like loyalty to est. And because of the implied and direct promises and because the $300 has already been paid, the enrollees accept and follow the rules.

According to firsthand reports on the leaders of the seminars, they are more like Gestapo agents than anything else. They often respond to trainees' disagreements or honest questions with intimidation and ridicule. The trainees are blitzkrieged out of their own belief system and bamboozled into the est belief system. Beliefs are not any good unless, of course, they are estian.

One leader is reported to have said, "We're gonna throw away your whole belief system. . . . We're gonna tear you down and put you back together." When one trainee asked about believing in something, he was interrupted by a leader who shouted, "Don't give me your goddamn belief system. . . . That doesn't work! That's why your whole life doesn't work." [71]

Mark Brewer reports one leader as saying to a group of trainees that they were "hopeless. They did not know what they were doing, did not know how to experience life, were struggling, desperate, confused. They were ASSHOLES!" [72] In fact, they were continually referred to as "assholes" throughout the training.

To pay $300 to have one's belief system ridiculed and replaced by one's own personal experience as the be-all and end-all of life is bad enough, but to keep on being referred to as an "asshole" on top of it should be more than anyone in his right mind would tolerate.

Another great "revelation" of est is that our minds are like machines. One leader declared, "You're a machine. *A machine!* Nothing but a goddamn machine!" [73] (Italics his.) So for $300 you not only get to be called an "asshole," but a "mechanical asshole."

After hours of this sort of haranguing, the leader suddenly comes to the rescue and gives his battered audience an exercise in meditation to show them how, in spite of the fact that they are only machines, they can control their own experience, "create their own space." Another exercise which the leader uses is very similar to Primal Therapy. This involves trainees lying on the floor and each experiencing his own experiences and feeling his own feelings. One advocate author of est describes it as: "Two hundred and fifty people in every form of emotion, giving free vent to vomiting, shaking, sobbing, hysterical laughing, raging." [74]

As the training draws to a close and reaches the proper pitch and crescendo, the individual learns that he is exactly the person that he wanted to be. He learns to accept the estian model of man as one who has freely chosen to be who and what he is. The trainee was only an "asshole" because he did not realize that he had truly chosen to be what he is.

If we don't acknowledge we're assholes because somewhere in

our belief systems we're hanging onto "it's bad to be an asshole," then we are really assholes. And it doesn't make any difference. An asshole is someone resisting being an asshole.[75]

Trainees are to realize through this training that they are perfect just the way they are. Erhard says, "I happen to think you are perfect exactly the way you are." [76]

Newsweek reports, "The culmination of the training comes when everyone realizes that he is free to transform experience through the prism of his own consciousness." [77] But, they "got it" after hours of being cajoled, then confused, and finally convinced. The result was more due to hours of harangue coupled with physical exhaustion, mental strain, and bloated bladders than to honest, rational assent. Only after hours of fatigue and deprivation along with boredom and irritation does the "enlightenment" occur.

In reporting her experience, one graduate said:

> For me it became boring, inane, exhausting. My chair became a jail cell. Of all the genius that had gone into est, I decided, the most ingenious was making people sit and do nothing and become aware of how hard it is to sit and do nothing.[78]

The same author-believer said that if she had not paid her nonrefundable fee in advance, she would not have returned after the first weekend.[79]

Est is a process of indoctrination and hypnotic suggestion induced by strange circumstances similar to that of an encounter marathon, during which one is reduced to a position of impotence and vulnerability without even realizing it. If it were not for the fact that people voluntarily take this training, it would easily qualify for the worst predictions of George Orwell's *1984*. If one were ever required to take such training against his will, est would be exposed for the brainwashing that it really is. Nevertheless, because it is voluntary brainwashing, it is considered an acceptable form of self help by its many advocates. Richard Farson expresses his concern:

> When people learn, as I believe they do in est, that it is acceptable, perhaps even necessary, to coerce, abuse, demean, incarcerate and exhaust people "for their own good" we have a

classic means/ends dilemma and, I'm afraid, the precondition for fascism.[80]

Nevertheless, the devotees of est far outnumber the ranks of dissatisfied customers. The devotion and loyalty to est that follows this quickie cure is amazing. It is reported that between 6,000 and 7,000 graduates do volunteer work for est each year.[81] The graduates' enthusiasm for est is evident in the high percentage of those who participate in graduate seminars.[82]

Does est really work? Is there such a thing as a quickie cure leading to fast, fast, fast relief? Can a person transform his life in two weekends? Are there long-term results from such a short-term experience? The testimonies of est graduates would strongly answer, "Yes." However, there is no research to support the testimonies. Nothing has been done with control groups, and, especially, no research has been conducted to evaluate positive change in behavior observed by others when the estians return to the real world.

Nevertheless, a public that will go for the ridiculousness of pet rocks will go for the unintelligible gibberish and psychogarble of "getting it." Est came along at the right time in history to fill the vacuum left by abandoning religious faith and by the unfulfilled promises of affluence. Est satisfies some obscure peculiarity caused by an inability to find meaning in life and a need to follow some guru or prophet.

Many have denied the one true Prophet to follow a farce. And many Christians have enrolled, oblivious to the false regeneration offered by this spurious system and its pretentious prophet. For example, one priest related after taking the training, "At est I got that I am satisfied with being the way I am. . . . est gave me the *experience* of what theology has been *telling* me. . . . I am much closer to God now." [83] (Italics his.)

Erhard has said, "God believed is a lie." [84] He also said, "Of all the disciplines that I studied, practiced, and learned, Zen was the *essential* one." [85] (Italics his.) One critic of est calls it "hardsell Zen." [86] Erhard avoids the God of the universe. Instead, he elevates human experience and makes a god out of self. One is not a sinner in the estian scheme; he is a saint. An estian believes in neither sin nor forgiveness, for he is supposedly perfect just the way he is. If one is perfect just the way he is, who needs atonement? And, who needs forgiveness? For after all, "I-I-I am perfect just the way I am."

Peter Marin refers to this in an article which he titled "The New Narcissism." He calls it "the trend in therapy toward a deification of the isolated self." [87] He further says, "The self replaces . . . God . . . so we now turn to self, giving to it the power and importance of a god." [88] Thus, the self-seeking man would rather be called a "mechanical asshole" than a sinner. He would rather swallow the placebo of "I'm the center of the universe" and "I'm great just the way I am" than accept the eternal truth of Scripture.

19. Arica

In the fourth polluted stream there are many spiritual psychologies, and Charles Tart discusses a number of them in his book *Transpersonal Psychologies*.[89] Many of the spiritual psychologies and systems of self-transformation are Eastern in origin. Daniel Goleman says, " . . . all the Eastern psychologies agree that the main means to this transformation of self is meditation." [90] Because these spiritual psychologies are more and more being included in Western psychotherapy someone once remarked, "The shrinks are beginning to sound like gurus, and the gurus are beginning to sound like shrinks." [91] Eastern religions and Western psychotherapy are becoming inseparable partners in the new fourth stream of psychology. We have selected Arica and Transcendental Meditation as two examples of the many spiritual psychotherapeutic systems available to the consumer.

Arica is a recent fourth-force psychotherapy invented by Oscar Ichazo. Although he has never advertised it as such, it is a form of existential psychotherapy. Yet, it is also a religion, and one might miss recognizing it as psychotherapy.

Ichazo was raised in Bolivia and Peru by Roman Catholic parents. As a young boy he went to a Jesuit school where he learned about the theology of the church. At the age of six Ichazo began to have epileptic-like attacks which involved much fear and pain. He claims that during these attacks he died, left his body, and later returned. He experienced both fear and ecstasy during these attacks, and because of these dramatic psychic experiences he became disillusioned with the church.

Neither heaven nor hell as described by the church matched his own psychic experiences, which he trusted more than the teachings of the church. Although he at first tried to deal with his unusual experiences through communion and prayer, he soon turned away from the church, because he felt that prayer caused him to focus even more on his problem. At this point, Ichazo left the way of grace and looked to his own experiences as the epicenter of reality. He relinquished the biblical forms of supernatural communication and relied upon self as the center of understanding.

During the following years, he studied and became actively involved in the martial arts, Zen, psychedelic drugs, shamanism, hypnotism and yoga. At 19 he became attached to an older man in La Paz who taught him much of what Ichazo calls truth. This man regularly met with a small group of men to share their knowledge of various esoteric techniques. Ichazo was present at these meetings and eventually these men began to teach him their secret knowledge. Later Ichazo traveled and studied in Hong Kong, India, and Tibet. He expanded his training in the martial arts and yoga and studied Buddhism, Confucianism, and the I Ching.

After his travels, he returned to La Paz to live with his father and to digest all he had learned. A year later he went into what he calls "a divine coma." After seven days of this coma he knew that he should be a teacher. Two years later Ichazo went to Santiago and lectured in the Institute for Applied Psychology. From there he moved to the remote little town of Arica, Chile, where he worked with a small committed group of followers.

Later, in 1970, a group of Americans went to Arica to study with him for nine months. During this time he decided to move his work to North America, and in 1971 he opened the Arica Institute in New York. Since then, the movement has expanded with centers in Los Angeles and San Francisco, as well as in New York, and with training programs in numerous other cities. Over 200,000 individuals have taken the Arica training.[92]

Arica distinguishes between man as he is in essence and man as he is in ego. Ichazo teaches that in essence every person is perfect and no conflict exists within the person or between one person and another. He contends that everyone begins life in pure essence, but that as the ego begins to develop man falls from essence to ego. Ichazo claims that the purity of essence is lost between four and six years of age. As a result of the civilizing and acculturating process, a contradiction occurs between the child's inner feelings and societal demands for conformity. Ego arises out of this conflict and stands between the world and the self.

Ichazo defines ego as composed of intellectual, emotional and movement segments that are interconnected. He says that ego is the fundamental human problem. Thus, the goal of Arica is ego reduction. According to Ichazo, when we turn away from our essence or self, we become dependent upon things external to us. We become driven by desire and fear with the ego always existing in fear, because it has created a subjective inner world that must be defended against objective reality. When desire is purged, a person returns to his essence and only then is true happiness realized.[93]

Arica supposedly trains people to think with their entire bodies rather than just with their minds. To facilitate such thinking, Arica provides a system of twelve mantations, each of which corresponds to a different part of the body. For instance, orientation is in the genitals, charisma in the knees and elbows, etc. Thus, thought is not restricted to only one organ of the body, the brain. In fact, as the ego becomes extinguished, thought is less an activity of the head and becomes a product of the various parts of the body. Once this happens, the head is emptied and stops controlling everything. Arica trains one to be less head oriented and more body oriented.

Arica assigns three centers to the individual: the intellectual, the emotional, and the vital. They are known as the path, the oth and the kath. Arica attempts to place kath, or body center, at the helm. This body center was first located four inches below the navel. However, a call to the Los Angeles Arica center revealed that the location has apparently moved from four inches to four fingers, or about three inches, below the navel.

In order to transfer consciousness from path (head) to kath (so-called body center), Arica uses enneagrams, which are circles with nine points on the circumference and which are used to analyze ego types, movement, breathing, and mantras. When the ego is completely exposed and finally destroyed through Arica techniques, the essence is to quite naturally take over. Ichazo claims that as the ego develops, Karma in the form of the evils of money, power and sex accumulate, and therefore the destruction of the ego is imperative to restore purity.

Each exercise and activity of Arica training aims at the goal of Permanent 24, which is a so-called state of total awareness, a state of higher consciousness to which all Arica followers aspire but none has yet attained. It is an illusive peak experience described. and promoted by Arica, but never yet achieved.

There are certain similarities between Arica and Christianity that make it attractive to many. The fall of man from essence to ego as described by Ichazo has all the earmarks of the Garden of Eden experience. It provides a substitute explanation for the fallen condition of man and, therefore, appeals to what man honestly knows is true.

The description of the ego sounds like the biblical doctrine of self-centeredness and sin. The desire of the ego, as described by Ichazo, sounds like the natural condition of man as a result of the Fall: man as sinner. The destruction of the ego and the path to Permanent 24 sounds like the process of biblical sanctification, which is the process of becoming like Jesus. It is the process of Christian maturity which involves the destruction of self-centeredness, and yet perfection is never fully realized in our present existence.

Nevertheless, Ichazo claims that he is not starting a new religion and that Arica is not a church, even though he has included important ideas from Buddhist, Taoist, Islamic, and Christian sources. He says that the techniques, which do come from a variety of religious and esoteric sources, provide experiences, but that there is no dogma and no creed as there is in a religion. People are merely asked to try the techniques and experience the results. However, doctrine and faith are both obviously involved.

Ichazo even has his own brand of eschatology. He says that humanity faces a crisis in the near future and that the way to avert it is through attaining a new level of consciousness. This level of consciousness is attained, of course, through Arica training. This gives the leaders and participants a self-righteous reason for the training. They are not just helping themselves; they are helping all of mankind.

Ichazo's out-of-the-body experiences as a child resulted in his disillusionment with the church and rejection of communion and prayer. He replaced these with his own psychic experiences and with such doctrines as reincarnation. In place of Christianity, he set up a new psychotherapy, a new religion, and a new method of spiritual renewal. His use of Eastern meditative techniques in combination with astrology, Gestalt, and encounter makes Arica a brand of psychotherapy. His use of divine consciousness as a universal god concept makes Arica a religion, but his use of words like God and Holy Spirit do not make Arica acceptable to Christianity. Unfortunately, Ichazo has given up communion with the true and living God to worship at strange altars.

20. Transcendental Meditation

Of all the meditation movements and spiritual psychologies available to the Western consumer, Transcendental Meditation (trademarked also as TM) is the most highly publicized and propagated. TM, like Arica, is another combination of religion and psychotherapy, although denying to be either, which promises a panacea for everyone.

Maharishi Mahesh Yogi is the founder of Transcendental Meditation. He learned the technique in India from his mentor, Guru Dev. Following the death of Guru Dev, Maharishi experienced two years of solitude after which he began to teach his method from town to town in India. While still in

India in 1961, he conducted his first TM teacher training course. Then in 1965, as a result of student response to local courses at UCLA, the Maharishi formed the Students' International Meditation Society (SIMS). The second teacher training course was again conducted in India in 1966, and in 1967 the Maharishi lectured at meetings on the Berkeley, UCLA, Harvard, and Yale campuses. This series of lectures was the impetus for establishing SIMS chapters all over the United States.

From these campuses, the practice of TM extended into the communities, and other organizations were developed to serve these new converts. By the close of 1970, about 35,000 Americans had learned TM, and in 1974 the report was that "300,000 Americans have learned to meditate, and 15,000 more start TM every month." [94] In 1976, *Newsweek* reported 800,000 meditators, but current reports claim nearly one million practitioners of TM in America and almost two million worldwide.

The goal of the leaders of the movement is to have meditators throughout the entire world. *Brain/Mind* reports that the Maharishi has begun his most ambitious project called the "global initiative." It is "a crash program to get three to four percent of the population meditating in specific states, cities and provinces around the world." [95]

TM is now used regularly by people from every walk of life, from playwrights to professors and from artists to astronauts. What is this method that is proliferating in America and aspires to saturate the world? The authors of *TM Discovering Inner Energy and Overcoming Stress*, which, incidentally, is 290 pages of promotional advertising, claim, "TM can be learned in a few hours and is then practiced for only fifteen to twenty minutes each morning and evening. The technique is a specific method of allowing the activity of the mind to settle down while one sits comfortably with eyes closed." [96]

They try to assure the reader that TM is "neither a religion or a philosophy, nor a way of life," but that it is "a natural technique for reducing stress and expanding conscious awareness." [97] The meditator learns to disengage himself from his surroundings and to allow his attention to shift inward. This eventually draws him into the peak experience of TM called "pure awareness," which "consists of nothing more than being wide awake inside without being aware of anything except awareness itself." [98] Such meditation supposedly provides a means of achieving pure awareness twice a day.

The mantra is an important part of the TM technique and plays a vital role in the whole meditative experience. The mantras, thought-sounds used by TMers, do not have any particular meaning. They are used for their hypnotic sound quality rather than for their meaning, because a pleasant sound is more easily focused upon and can be somewhat soothing. There is much ado about the selection, assignment, and use of mantras in TM. There is supposed to be just the right mantra for each person and meditators are warned not to choose their own mantras but to have qualified teachers assign them and instruct in their correct usage.

TM claims that mantras are chosen individually according to personality type. However, R. D. Scott, a former TM teacher and author of *Transcendental Misconceptions*,[99] says that mantras are chosen according to age and sex. Nevertheless, each student believes that the mantra assigned specifically to him is very special and individual, and he is not to reveal it to anyone. This creates an air of importance and secrecy and also protects the meditators from learning that their own special mantra is not so special after all. Furthermore, the meditator is more likely to pay attention to his own private mantra than to one that is common to others. Thus, whenever unpleasant distractions occur, he can quickly focus on his own pleasant sounding, "special," private mantra, but only if he has been especially trained by a TM instructor and given the secret formula.

The mantra is extremely important in achieving the so-called fourth state of awareness in which one arrives at the very "source of thought." This is also called the fourth state of consciousness in relation to the other major states—those of waking, sleeping, and dreaming. Robert Ornstein gives a simple explanation for this experience. He believes that when a person concentrates on a single stimulus like a mantra, it reduces his attention to other stimuli, and then with repetition the single stimulus disappears leaving an awareness of nothing. It is attention without content and what TMers call "pure consciousness." In this regard there is nothing special about TM, because any nonobjectionable repetitive stimulus will cause similar reactions in people. If a person concentrates long enough on a single neutral object, certain biological results occur, including dissociation from the external world.[100]

One basic premise of TM is that it enables a person to regulate the states of consciousness in order to feel better. However, TM is only one of many meditation disciplines used to influence consciousness. Its great advantage over other approaches in the marketplace is that it is simple to do and requires a minimal amount of training. Gary Schwartz mentions Zen, Sufi, Christian meditation, autogenic training, and progressive relaxation and declares that any of these kinds of activities may bring deep and helpful rest.[101]

There is no question that a person can regulate his own states of consciousness, but he can do this in a number of ways without TM. For example, the alpha and theta brain waves which are associated with relaxation and drowsiness can be influenced by merely focusing and unfocusing the eyes. In addition to influencing brain waves, one can breathe or think in certain ways to influence consciousness.

TM makes numerous claims, including: *increased* intelligence, learning ability, creativity, energy level, sociability, capacity for intimate contact, emotional stability, self-confidence, resistance to disease, balance of the autonomic nervous system, etc.; *reduced* anxiety, irritability, antisocial behavior, depression, neuroticism, crime rate, use of alcohol and cigarettes, etc.[102]

TM claims all kinds of physiological and psychological improvement and attempts to support these claims with research by biased believers. For instance, Robert Wallace, past president of the Maharishi International University, tabulated various physiological responses to TM. Besides the increase in alpha and theta waves, he noted a drop in oxygen consumption, which would reveal lowered metabolism, and a rise in skin resistance, which would mean an increased state of arousal.

Such findings, as well as others that supposedly indicate changes in blood chemistry, suggest that TM enhances relaxation and reduces stress. However, Ornstein contends that recorded brain-wave changes are not reliable indicators of altered brain functions unless there are extremely strict research controls.[103] According to Leon Otis, those who conducted physiological studies on TM at the Stanford Research Institute believe that simple resting at regular intervals may bring about as much bodily change as meditation.[104] Gary Schwartz warns that "we should remain wary of the claims and selective use of scientific data by well-meaning but scientifically unsophisticated practitioners." [105]

A highly controversial claim made for TM is that it increases creativity and intelligence. However, Schwartz compared a group of teachers of meditation with a control group using two standardized measures of creativity. He reported that the results were similar for both groups, except that the meditators did consistently worse on some scales even though they were highly motivated to succeed.[106] Another study conducted at the University of Illinois indicated that TM did not result in higher academic performance on the part of typical students who simply took the TM training.[107]

Leon Otis and his associates at the Stanford Research Institute conducted a series of experiments on TM which did show some advantages for the meditation group over the control group. However, after the interviews were conducted, Otis reported:

> . . . the meditators had expected greater gains than the controls had. I feel certain, then, that a placebo effect was partly responsible for the benefits the meditators finally claimed.[108]

Gary Schwartz also believes that expectation plays a large role in bringing about positive results from the TM experience.[109] Thus, it may be that TM is a sugarcoated pill, easy to swallow and easier to believe. Faith in TM enhances its effectiveness.

The claim that TM is not a religion is attacked by Dan Goleman, associate editor of *Psychology Today*. He says:

> Such an assertion ignores the fact that TM grew out of the mystical Advaita school of yoga and uses a Hindu devotional as an initiation ritual. Avoiding religious or philosophical

issues keeps Catholic, Protestant, and Jewish customers comfortable.[110]

Judge H. Curtis Meanor ruled that the teaching of TM in the New Jersey public high schools violated the constitutional guarantee of the separation of church and state. Like any religious cult, TM claims to have special knowledge and to produce special results. It claims unique knowledge about consciousness and extraordinary psychological and physiological results. Moreover, TM initiates are given secret codes and mystical mantras.

TM is both a form of relaxation and a religion. It is a mistake to assume that because it involves relaxing techniques that it is not a religion. We object less to TM as a form of relaxation than to its disguised religious nature. However, even as a form of relaxation, one must be careful not to generalize about its effectiveness. Schwartz warns that excessive practice of TM could have negative side effects. He says, "A few people, with a tendency toward mental illness, may even aggravate their condition by meditating for long periods." [111]

Man is really a spiritual being and will sometimes seek a psychological salvation as an alternate to the spiritual salvation that he really needs. TM provides a pseudosolution to the spiritual sickness of man. One is supposedly saved by attaining pure consciousness. Maharishi teaches that through TM "a sinner comes out of the field of sin and becomes a virtuous man." [112] According to the Bible, we are saved by Christ, not by meditation.

As a religion or a psychotherapy, TM must be rejected by the Christian as a substitute means of grace and peace. Rather than emptying his mind with a repetitive mantra, the Christian would do well to fill his mind with the Word of God and fix his mind on the character and love of his Creator.

> Blessed is the man that walketh not in the counsel of the ungodly, nor standeth in the way of sinners, nor sitteth in the seat of the scornful. But his delight is in the law of the Lord; and in his law doth he meditate day and night. (Ps. 1:1, 2)

> My soul shall be satisfied as with marrow and fatness: and my mouth shall praise thee with joyful lips: when I remem-

ber thee upon my bed, and meditate on thee in the night watches. (Ps. 63:5, 6)

21. Strange Altars

Throughout the history of psychotherapy we have seen the rise and wane of one therapy after another, one promise after another, one hope of success after another, and one polluted psychological stream after another. We have swung 180° through four forces of psychotherapy from Freud's rejection of religion as an illusion to new combinations of psychic religion and fetish. We have moved from a dependency upon the natural world as being the sole reality in life to a rejection of it as only an illusion.

John Wren-Lewis says:

> As psychotherapy spreads into society at large, it becomes increasingly suffused with ideas and techniques derived from mysticism and occultism.[113]

These include such activities as meditation, yoga, Actualism, astrology, Tarot, spiritism, and mystic initiation rites, all offered as means of expanding awareness. Theodore Roszak, in his book *Unfinished Animal: The Aquarian Frontier and the Evolution of Consciousness*, sees the whole consciousness revolution as mankind's only hope of survival.[114] Sam Keen, a consulting editor of *Psychology Today*, reports:

> If the prophets and gurus of the consciousness revolution are to be believed, God has been reborn and we are rapidly approaching the Omega Point, the Great Awakening, the New Age of the Spirit.[115]

Robert Ornstein describes the contemporary psychotherapeutic scene as follows:

> Gurus, the promise of instant enlightenment, and degenerate versions of Eastern spiritual traditions seem to have replaced church and temple for many Americans. People flock unthinkingly to quick, cheap and flashy spiritual sideshows, hoping for happiness, self-awareness, and inner peace.[116]

Newsweek reports that the whole consciousness

> . . . movement has created a network of therapeutic outlets

servicing millions of Americans who are bored, dissatisfied with their lives or seeking a God they can experience for themselves.[117]

It is interesting to note that during the period of time that Christianity was becoming less and less experience oriented, psychotherapy was becoming more and more experience oriented.

We now have a new religious psychotherapy on the scene that is a religion without a creed and a faith without a personal God. Though it is an antidote for materialism, it ignores demonism. It denies the absolutes of Scripture and establishes a divinity of self. It stresses the innate goodness of man and usually rejects the fallen condition and nature of man. It is a poor substitute for Christianity but has been accepted by those who have rejected or not known the truth. Man has a spiritual vacuum at his very core and it must be filled if he is to be whole. The fourth force in psychotherapy is only a substitute for the reality of God.

Many have run from religion until the emptiness finally caught up with them, and now, instead of returning to the one true God of the universe, they are following the false gods of men's minds. Instead of looking to God, the creator of man, many are looking to man the creator of gods and end up replacing one vacuum with another. Robert Ornstein has well said, "Our culture is the best educated, wealthiest, most 'emotionally aware' in history. It is also one of the most spiritually illiterate." [118]

22. *Whited Sepulchers*

Christians have been attracted to one or more of the preceding psychotherapies, as well as to numerous other brands not even mentioned in this book. However, there are certain psychotherapies which are particularly appealing to Christians.

Second Corinthians says that "Satan himself is transformed into an angel of light. Therefore, it is no great thing if his ministers also be transformed as the ministers of righteousness: whose end shall be according to their works" (11:14, 15). An angel of light is one who appears to be righteous but is really not. Jesus used the expression "whited sepulchers" to describe the scribes and Pharisees. They seem beautiful on the outside but are filled with dead men's bones.

Some of the psychotherapies are like this. They seem to be very Christian in doctrine and principle, but on closer examination they contain only the ideas of men. Some of them even contain a "form of godliness," but, as the Scriptures say, "they lack the power thereof." Because they resemble Christianity on the surface, Christians fall for them in the same way that some are led astray by religious cults. We have selected a few such "angels of light" for discussion. They are Client-Centered Therapy, developed by Carl Rogers; Reality Therapy by William Glasser; and Transactional Analysis, originated by Eric Berne and popularized by Thomas Harris.

These psychotherapies appeal to Christians because of their emphasis upon free will, personal responsibility, and a form of morality. On the surface they all sound great and there would be general agreement among these men on many ideas. Listen, be real, and love (Rogers); reality, responsibility, and right-and-wrong (Glasser); and I'M OK—YOU'RE OK (Harris) seem like gold, silver, and precious stones. However, all involve self at the center. Self is elevated and a new catechism of cure is preached, which is based upon me, myself, and I. Paul predicted: "This know also, that in the last days perilous times shall come. For men shall be lovers of their own selves, covetous, boasters, proud, blasphemers, disobedient to parents, unthankful, unholy" (2 Tim. 3:1, 2).

Theodore Roszak was quoted in *Newsweek* as saying that America is launched on "the biggest introspective binge any society in history has undergone." [1] All of these angels of light elevate self and they do it with finesse. They disguise self-love and self-indulgence with such terms as I'M OK—YOU'RE OK and "self-actualization." They all deny the authority of the Bible and distort biblical truths. Nevertheless, even though they promise hope for the future, their substance is only wood, hay, and stubble.

23. Client-Centered Therapy

One of the best-known and most admired humanistic psychologists today is Carl Rogers. Rogers has spent a lifetime studying human behavior and has developed a technique of treatment called "nondirective" or "client-centered" therapy. It is nondirective in that the therapist does not lead the client's attention to any topic or material. The client does the choosing. It is client-centered in that it proposes to allow the client to have his own insights and to make his own interpretations rather than looking to the therapist to provide the insights and interpretations.

Jay Haley says, "Actually nondirective therapy is a misnomer. To state that any communication between two people can be nondirective is to state an impossibility." [2] A therapist, even without intending to do so, will influence what his client thinks, says, and does.[3]

Rogers developed a theory of personality called the "self theory," which assumes that everyone has the ability to change and that everyone has a measure of freedom for self-direction and growth. He places great importance on the uniqueness of the individual. His view of the basic nature of man is positive and is a welcome contrast to the negative and deterministic view of man presented by both the psychoanalytic and behavioristic models.

The self theory with its positive possibilities came at a time in history when we were facing material affluence but experiencing spiritual emptiness. This theory seemed to fill the emptiness and provide new hope to match the new affluence. It emphasized the kind of personal values and self-determination which permitted one to enjoy the material prosperity more fully.

Besides emphasizing the innate goodness of man, Rogers sees self as central, in that each person lives in his own special world of experience, in which he is the center and forms his own judgments and values. Although Rogers places strong emphasis upon values for guiding behavior and for living a meaningful life, he says that these values should be based upon internal, individual decisions rather than blind acceptance of the values in one's environment. All experiences in self theory are evaluated in relation to the individual's self concept.

Rogers believes that a person's inner tendencies are toward what he calls "self-actualization," which he identifies as the basic force motivating the person. Through self-actualization, the person tries to maintain his personhood and strives to grow towards a greater sense of fulfillment in relation to his self concept and in relation to how other people relate to him. Rogers believes that the natural man's basic inner direction is towards health and wholeness.

Rogers and Christianity

Important to Rogers' self theory is his view of Christianity.

Christianity was not foreign to Rogers. He describes himself as "the middle child in a large, close-knit family, where hard work and a highly conservative Protestant Christianity were about equally revered." [4] At one time he attended Union Theological Seminary and he confesses that during a seminar he, as well as others, "thought themselves right out of religious work." [5] He felt that on the one hand he would probably always be interested in the "questions as to the meaning of life," [6] but on the other hand he says, "I could not work in a field where I would be required to believe in some specified religious doctrine." [7] Obviously he sees Christianity as having requirements rather than privileges.

Rogers goes on to say, "I wanted to find a field in which I could be sure my freedom of thought would not be limited." [8] Rogers does not want to be what he calls "limited" by biblical dogma, but by his very act he has set up another kind of dogma. Instead of an external dogma (Bible), he has set up an internal dogma (self). He has restricted himself by the very act of refusing Christianity. His refusal of Christian doctrine placed restrictions upon his own thought and influenced his entire work.

We will first examine how his rejection of Christianity colors his theories; then we will consider three important ideas which he discovered during his career and compare them with biblical principles. Basically, some of Rogers' theory and therapy is soundly biblical, without giving credit to the Bible, but other parts are absolutely contrary to Scripture.

Rogers received enough Christianity to deny determinism but not enough to escape self-indulgence. He rejected the external authority of Scripture and established an internal authority of self. This rejection changed the course of his career from theology to psychology and from the worship of God to the worship of self. He exalts self rather than God. The apostle Paul describes this move from serving God to serving self in the first chapter of Romans. Paul says that men "changed the truth of God into a lie, and worshipped and served the creature more than the Creator" (Rom. 1:25).

Rogers is to be commended for his break with psychoanalytic and behavioristic determinism, but not for his self theory.

Steeped in the philosophy of humanism, Rogers believes in the basic goodness of man, and his system establishes the self as the final authority rather than God. His avoidance of "religious dogma" is a rejection of external authority and places self at the center of all experience. Although Rogers stresses freedom of choice, the basis for such a choice is the internal value system of the individual, rather than the external authority of Scripture. The value system focuses upon the earthly and immediate rather than on the heavenly and eternal. It is based upon the natural without regard to the supernatural and divine.

For the Christian, the Word of God is supreme; for the self theorist the word of self is supreme. And when the self is thus exalted, the biblical concept of sin goes out the window and is replaced by another concept of sin, which is based upon the standards established by self. Although Rogers can be commended for recognizing the uniqueness of man, he rejects the universality of sin.

The concept of self-actualization sounds quite lofty and wonderful, but it is merely a disguise for self-indulgence. Self theory has self at the center of all things, and this position of the self has been and always will be contrary to Scripture. We live in a God-centered (theocentric) universe with theocratic rule, not in a self-centered (egocentric) universe with egocratic rule.

Rogers' Three "Discoveries"

Carl Rogers claims to have discovered three important principles during his lifetime of studying human behavior and practicing his therapy.[9] The first principle is that of listening. He points out that people have a real need to be heard and that seemingly unbearable problems become bearable when someone listens. He further believes that a sense of utter loneliness occurs when no one listens.

There is no question that listening is a vital response. However, this "fact of psychotherapy," newly "discovered" by Rogers, was long known and used by the church. James wrote to the early church, " . . . let every man be swift to hear, slow to speak, slow to wrath" (James 1:19). This is a necessary function of every man, not a special gift given to only a few chosen persons.

Rogers did discover something of infinite value, but it was a fact of Scripture long before it became a fact of psychotherapy. We need not follow Carl Rogers into the web of self theory just because of one truth which already existed in Scripture. Furthermore, Rogers completely omits the crucial concept of listening to God and of His response of listening to our words, our thoughts, and our unspoken yearnings.

Rogers' second important principle is "to be real." By this he means being oneself and not playing a role or being phony. Being honest with oneself and others is also a principle found throughout Scripture. For instance, the writer of Hebrews says, "Pray for us: for we trust we have a good conscience, in all things willing to live honestly" (Heb. 13:18). Paul exhorted the Thessalonians to "walk honestly" (1 Thess. 4:12) and he encouraged servants to serve "not with eyeservice, as menpleasers; but as the servants of Christ, doing the will of God from the heart" (Eph. 6:6). The Bible teaches that God looks upon the heart of man, the real inner person, and that men are to be honest and true. Being unreal is a form of deception and false witness; being unreal is labeled *sin* in the Bible.

Although both Rogers and the Bible encourage a person to be real, do the concepts of Rogers and the teachings of the Bible harmonize on this basic principle? If by "being real" Rogers means following whatever internal value system that one has developed, good or bad, his form of "being real" is not biblical truth; it is just another form of self-deception which could lead to disaster.

Attached to Rogers' principle "to be real" is his concept of "unconditional self-regard," which is merely a euphemism for self love. Rogers says that unconditional self-regard occurs when the person "perceives himself in such a way that no self-experience can be discriminated as more or less worthy of positive regard than any other." [10] According to Rogers, the individual becomes the "locus of evaluation," the final authority and evaluator of all experience.

After much research in the area of human judgment,

Einhorn and Hogarth point out the paradox of a person's high confidence in his own judgment in spite of its unreliability. They bemoan the fact that, because of a person's tendency to rely on his own fallible judgment, theories such as Rogers', which totally depend upon a person's subjective perception and evaluation, will continue to be popular.[11]

Rogers' system puts self in the position to say, "I am the one that evaluates all experiences and I am the one who sets up my own value system. Nothing is in and of itself more valuable than anything else unless I say so." This is surely contrary to Scripture, because it eliminates the Bible and sets up self as the center of authority and the creator of values. Rogers has rejected the biblical doctrine of being real and substituted a false doctrine, which eliminates the Bible as the source of truth and denies the biblical concept of sin.

Rogers' third important principle, which he considers to be his crowning discovery, is that of "love between persons." When Jesus was asked, "What is the greatest commandment?" He answered "love." He further said to His disciples, "Love one another, as I have loved you" (John 15:12). In addition, 1 Corinthians 13 ends: "And now abideth faith, hope, and love, these three; but the greatest of these is love." Love is one of the most obvious and repeated principles in all Scripture.

Before we criticize or compliment Rogers, we need to understand what he means by "love between persons." First of all, Rogers is only speaking about human love. While human love is an admirable virtue, it does not compare with divine love. Human love without the divine is merely another form of self love. Divine love, on the other hand, encompasses all the qualities listed in 1 Corinthians 13. Second, Rogers is only speaking of love between humans. He ignores the great commandment to "love the Lord thy God." Third, he never mentions God's love for man, which is demonstrated throughout the Bible.

Rogers' crowning discovery is a limited human love between persons, which excludes the love of God and the love for God. In excluding God, Rogers sets up the me, myself, and I as the evaluator and prioritizer of all experiences. The self, rather than God, becomes the center of the universe, and love apart from God becomes only a self-rewarding activity. In leaving out God, Rogers ends up with a "love between persons," which is hardly more than a feeble extension of self love.

Remember that these important ideas did not originate with Rogers. They have always existed. Rogers merely found three principles that are superficial substitutes for the deep divine principles of Scripture.

In both theory and therapy, Carl Rogers has managed to elevate self to the position of being a god. Paul C. Vitz has done an excellent job of comparing the self theory of Rogers with Christianity and of exposing it as a form of self worship in his book *Psychology As Religion: The Cult of Self Worship*.[12] With self at the center of the universe and God completely ignored, self theory exists as a counterfeit religion. Self theory, an influential system within the third polluted stream, wears an effective disguise. It sometimes looks like Christianity, but in reality it is often contrary to Scripture.

24. Reality Therapy

Reality Therapy is a radically non-Freudian type of therapy developed by psychiatrist William Glasser and described in his book *Reality Therapy*. The reality therapist is not interested in becoming involved in the two Freudian demons: the past history of the patient and the unconscious determinants of behavior.

Concerning the patient's past, Glasser says, " . . . we can neither change what happened to him nor accept the fact that he is limited by his past." [13] If a patient does mention the past, it is always to be related to the present and the future. Although Glasser believes in unconscious motivation for behavior, he says:

> . . . knowledge of cause has nothing to do with therapy. Patients have been treated with conventional psychiatry until they know the unconscious reason for every move they make, but they still do not change because knowing the reason does not lead to fulfilling needs.[14]

Furthermore, unconscious motivations are often just used as excuses for continuing undesirable behavior.

The core of Reality Therapy is found in the three R's—reality, responsibility, and right-and-wrong. These not only read like motherhood and apple pie, but they have a distinct Christian ring. Let's examine these three terms and the process of this therapy to see if Reality Therapy is indeed biblical.

Reality. Glasser stresses the importance of helping a person see and deal with life as it really is. A distorted view of the actions of other people, of the events affecting the person's life, and of one's own actions can lead to emotional problems and hinder that person from behaving in appropriate ways. Glasser believes that "all patients have a common characteristic: *they all deny the reality of the world around them.*" [15] (Italics his.) Thus, one main responsibility of the therapist is to bring the person in touch with the reality of his environment and of himself.

Glasser encourages his patients to develop behavior that is realistic in terms of both the present and the future. In doing this, he differentiates between immediate and long-range consequences of behavior. He points out that realistic behavior is that which results from a consideration of both long-range and short-range consequences, since some behavior, though immediately satisfying, may be unsatisfactory in the long run.

Responsibility. Glasser further says, " . . . it is not enough to help a patient face reality; he must also learn to fulfill his needs." [16] Responsibility, according to Glasser is "the ability to fulfill one's needs, and to do so *in a way that does not deprive others of the ability to fulfill their needs.*" [17] (Italics his.) Such behavior is the primary goal of Reality Therapy.

Glasser has an interesting notion about the relationship of behavior to human thought and emotions. He believes that people do not act responsibly just because they are happy, but rather that people who act responsibly are more likely to be happy. Happiness or the lack of it is thus dependent upon responsible behavior, rather than upon the circumstances in which a person finds himself. Therefore, the job of the therapist is to help people become responsible.

Although Glasser uses reason and logic in counseling, he does not concentrate heavily on either thoughts or emotions. Most psychotherapists try to change thoughts and emotions; but Glasser works directly with outward behavior. He believes that responsible behavior shapes positive thoughts and emotions, just as irresponsible behavior causes unhealthy attitudes and emotions.

There is an old saying that if you knew better you would do better. However, experience in life tends to disprove this, since people often do not perform according to what they know. Glasser's theory stresses doing better rather than just knowing better, for he believes that a change in behavior will lead to a change in thinking. Thus, he concentrates on teaching his patients responsible ways to respond.

Glasser not only holds the patient accountable for his own behavior, but refuses to take the responsibility away from him. Patients very often attempt to make others responsible for their behavior, but Reality Therapy denies them this privilege. Thus, the patient is both encouraged to perform responsibly and to be responsible for his performance. Glasser does not waste time asking why a person acted irresponsibly; instead, he assumes that the client can act responsibly and proceeds to help him do so.

Right-and-Wrong. The very idea of responsibility suggests morality of some kind, and, indeed, Reality Therapy includes the concept of right and wrong. Glasser says:

> . . . *to be worthwhile we must maintain a satisfactory standard of behavior*. To do so we must learn to correct ourselves when we do wrong and to credit ourselves when we do right. . . . Morals, standards, values, or right and wrong behavior are all intimately related to the fulfillment of our need for self worth.[18] (Italics his.)

Glasser's position is a refreshing contrast to most psychotherapies, which either stress the adverse effects of the moral standards of society on the individual or refuse to impose these, or any other standards, on the patient. In the Freudian system, a conscience which makes too many demands on the individual must be reformed to lower the moral expectations so that the person can feel good about himself.

Numerous psychotherapeutic systems encourage the individual to satisfy the instincts and impulses by reducing the demands of the conscience. These therapies are based on the theory that lowering the standards of conventional morality is beneficial and necessary for improved mental-emotional health. They focus on internal desires rather than external behavior. Glasser, on the other hand, does not believe in decreasing standards but, rather, in increasing performance. Reality Therapy devaluates the biological desires and elevates the social needs of the individual. It is a rare psychotherapeutic system that does this.

Process of Therapy

The duration of treatment with Reality Therapy is usually about six months and is rarely longer than a year. Of crucial importance in the process is the relationship between the therapist and the patient. Glasser believes that the therapist, as a person, provides the missing link to positive change. He says:

> We know, therefore, that *at the time any person comes for psychiatric help he is lacking the most critical factor for fulfilling his needs, a person whom he genuinely cares about and who he feels genuinely cares about him*.[19] (Italics his.)

In Reality Therapy the therapist must become this special person to whom the patient can respond.

Glasser believes that without involvement, there can be no therapy. The therapist must be both a friend to the patient and a model of responsibility for the patient to follow. As a friend he is to exhibit compassion and a caring attitude, but he is not to respond to unnecessary demands for sympathy nor react to criticism from the patient. Ideally the relationship becomes the motivation for responsible behavior.

Throughout therapy the major goal is to teach the patient to become responsible. As such, the therapist becomes a teacher as well as a friend. Thus, the therapist rejects irresponsible, unrealistic, and wrong behavior, but at the same time he maintains an attitude of accepting the patient himself. In fact, the therapist makes it clear that he will never reject the client, no matter what he does. Rather, it is the behavior that he rejects and that only for the ultimate good of the patient.

Through acceptance of the person and rejection of negative behavior, the therapist tries to help the patient evaluate his own behavior. The therapist also attempts to help his client to make plans for change and gives suggestions for carrying out the plans. Glasser claims that through this process, the patient develops more realistic and responsible behavior and thus finds self-fulfillment and happiness.

Criticisms of Reality Therapy

Well, what can be wrong with Reality Therapy? It sounds wholesome, good, and even biblical with such concepts as reality, responsibility, and right-and-wrong. Let's examine this seemingly virtuous system in the light of the Bible.

According to Glasser the individual has two basic psychological needs. He says they are *"the need to love and be loved and the need to feel that we are worthwhile to ourselves and to others."* [20] (Italics his.) While it is true that we have a "need to love and be loved," this concept is lacking in that it only emphasizes human relationships and totally ignores a person's need to have a loving relationship with God.

The Bible says, "We love him, because he first loved us" (1 John 4:19). God's love for us is so great that He gave His Son that we might have eternal life, and therefore we love Him. Jesus taught that the greatest commandment is, "And thou shalt love the Lord thy God with all thy heart, and with all thy soul, and with all thy mind, and with all thy strength" (Mark 12:30). The love relationship between God and man is one of the greatest doctrines of the entire Bible. It is of supreme importance to man and is a powerful force in the life of an individual. It has immeasurable therapeutic value and is of far greater value than love between men. In fact, our human love relationships are far better and more complete when our supernatural love is a reality.

Glasser, like Rogers, deals only with a natural love relationship and not the divine love relationship. Just as Rogers, Glasser emphasizes the need for caring and involvement between persons, but ignores man's greatest need for a love relationship with God.

Along with the need for love, Glasser noted that people need to feel worthwhile to themselves and to others. He says that although this need is separate from the first need, the person who satisfies the need to love and be loved will usually feel worthwhile. This sounds like a beautiful generalization, but here again it is incomplete and ignores the Bible. The important word in this second need is *feel*. A man can feel worthwhile under a variety of circumstances. He may even feel worthwhile because he loves and is loved. However, no one can BE worthwhile outside of a relationship with God.

The apostle Paul confessed in his letter to the Philippians that he had considered himself a very worthwhile individual, for not only did he have the exact right heritage, but he had followed the Jewish law and customs with great zeal and righteousness. However, when he came face to face with the resurrected Christ, he discovered that all he had considered worthy in himself was empty, because he had not been in the proper relationship with God. And from that point, he desired to "be found in him, not having mine own righteousness, which is of the law, but that which is through the faith of Christ, the righteousness which is of God by faith" (Phil. 3:9). Paul moved from *thinking* himself worthwhile to *being* worthwhile.

Feeling worthwhile is merely an internal evaluation, which might not be at all realistic. A person may feel he is worthwhile and establish his own system for saving the world and end up like Hitler. *Feeling* has to do with self, while *being* has to do with Scripture.

Using these two needs of men, Glasser defines moral behavior as, "*When a man acts in such a way that he gives and receives love, and feels worthwhile to himself and others, his behavior is right or moral.*" [21] (Italics his.) Nevertheless, if a man does not have a love relationship with God, he cannot truly be a worthwhile person in the biblical sense. The behavior he exhibits may or may not be scripturally moral. Although a man acting in the natural can feel worthwhile, the resulting behavior will not necessarily be moral according to biblical standards. Glasser's concept places an undue amount of confidence in man.

Glasser exhibits confidence in man because of his humanistic ideology, which says that men are basically good in themselves and which denies the fundamental nature of sinful, fallen man. We can expect both moral and immoral behavior from persons because of their fallen nature. Glasser would call immoral behavior "irresponsible," but it would be more appropriate to call it "sinful." Glasser cares more about the so-called rights and liberties of persons than about godly righteousness, religious beliefs, or the true freedom which can be found only in Jesus.

Glasser's system of therapy centers directly on behavior, but he completely ignores the Bible, which is filled with exhortations to behave wisely and responsibly, and substitutes it with the existing moral code. For example, if two people are in love and wish to live together without the commitment of marriage, they would certainly be conforming to Glasser's definition of responsible behavior, since it fulfills their needs, does not deprive or restrict others from fulfilling their needs, and fits into current moral practices. But the Bible is opposed to such relationships, and responsible Christian behavior conforms to the Word of God.

Societal standards, the laws of men, and the prevailing moral code change, but the law of God is eternal. What is the sense of responsible behavior that is limited to outward conformity to a current moral code if it is divorced from an internal change caused by the supernatural presence of God? Glasser is more concerned with outward behavior than with the inner attitude, but God looks on the heart rather than the external appearance. For Glasser it doesn't matter what you believe as long as you act according to current mores. The Bible deals with the whole man, with his inner and outer behavior.

Although men can change their behavior to a certain extent, they are nevertheless restricted by the inherent tendency to sin because of the fallen nature. Only God's grace enables a person to act fully responsible, and even then there are slips and sins that have to be forgiven.

Paul expressed this quandry in Romans 7 when he said that with the mind he wanted to do the right thing, but he did just the opposite anyway because of the sin principle within him. He found that the power to act responsibly, both inwardly and outwardly, was only through allowing Jesus to be Lord in his life and through the power of the indwelling Holy Spirit. Throughout the entire Old Testament, the Israelites were unable to follow the law of God. However, when Jesus came and gave His life for men, He enabled them to receive His own perfect life. He transforms their hearts and lives so that they can be new creatures in both inner and outward behavior.

When one closely examines Glasser's view of reality, responsibility, and right-and-wrong, he sees a worldly system which sounds somewhat biblical, but is not. Besides failing to conform to the Bible, Reality Therapy proposes to heal mental-emotional disorders through self-effort. Like nearly all psychotherapies, self, not God, is at the center of Reality Therapy. It is a system that uses biblical sounding concepts like love and worthwhileness, and yet it uses them in a shallow, self-centered, human sense. Ingredients necessary to dissolve mental-emotional disorders are biblical love, the biblical way to worthwhileness, and biblically responsible behavior, not the three R's of Glasser.

Christians have been deceived by a system that relies upon worldly standards of reality, responsibility, and right-and-wrong. The Bible describes reality and teaches responsibility and right and wrong behavior. Although Glasser is close to the truth, he has struck out on all three since his concepts are non-biblical, worldly, and self-oriented.

According to Reality Therapy, the therapist is the model for the patient to follow in order to attain the goal of responsible behavior. On the other hand, the Bible teaches that Christ is the model and our goal is to be like Him. Spiritual counseling presents Christ, not the therapist; Christ, not fallen nature; Christ, not self. One who provides help based on the Bible will constantly refer to and exhibit scriptural love, mercy, and grace, as well as scriptural reality, responsibility, and right and wrong. The biblical counselor will use Christ as the model and Christ's overcoming victory as the example, rather than himself and his own ability. These are the only truly valid and reliable mental health principles for men because they have been given by the One who created us. Christians would do well to stay away from even biblical sounding therapies and return to the Word, which is the Christian source of all mental-emotional healing and health.

25. Transactional Analysis

Transactional Analysis (TA) is a therapeutic system which is used primarily with groups and which examines interactions between people. To understand the weaknesses of Transactional Analysis, let us examine some of its concepts, its four life positions, and its unproven theories.

Thomas Harris, in his best seller *I'M OK—YOU'RE OK: A Practical Guide to Transactional Analysis*, quotes the work of neurosurgeon Wilder Penfield and offers it as a basis for his own theory. Under the influence of Penfield, Harris believes that both past events and the feelings which accompanied those events are recorded in the brain in such a way that each event is forever united with the emotion. According to Harris, the events and emotions remain linked together in the brain throughout life. Harris refers to the brain as a high fidelity tape recorder and uses this metaphor to describe his system. He constantly refers to events being recorded or played back.

Harris says that during his early years a child is recording volumes of negative feelings, which greatly influence his entire life. These negative recordings come from certain demands which are imposed upon him and which are accompanied by parental approval or disapproval. Toilet training is one example. During this time the child has a need to empty his bowels and the parent has a need to eventually train him. Thus, there is often a conflict between what the child is doing and what the parent wants him to do.

Harris says that negative feelings from the civilizing process bring a child to the conclusion that he is NOT OK. Harris is not necessarily blaming the parents, for he says, "It is the *situation of childhood* and *not* the intention of the parents which produces the problem." [22] (Italics his.) Even the child of loving parents comes to the same conclusion according to Harris.

Four Life Positions

Harris does indicate that the child receives OK recordings as well as NOT OK ones, but he believes that the NOT OK feelings predominate.[23] His belief in the universal NOT OK experience of mankind is the key to TA and to his four life positions, which are:

I'M NOT OK—YOU'RE OK
I'M NOT OK—YOU'RE NOT OK
I'M OK—YOU'RE NOT OK
I'M OK—YOU'RE OK

The first position, I'M NOT OK—YOU'RE OK, is established by a decision made by every young child. The child concludes that he is NOT OK because the NOT OK feelings ultimately outweigh the OK feelings. He concludes that the parent is OK because the parent provides what Harris labels "stroking," which is "repetitious bodily contact." [24] The child evaluates the goodness of the parent through the amount of stroking he receives. Since the parents, and particularly the mother, provide stroking, the child concludes YOU'RE OK. Harris says that the conclusion I'M NOT OK—YOU'RE OK is the "universal position of early childhood" and is "the most deterministic decision of his life." [25]

If there is an absence of necessary stroking, the child moves from position one to life position two: I'M NOT OK—YOU'RE NOT OK. This is a position of abandonment and despair and the beginning of deep mental-emotional problems. There is no hope because no one is OK. Often a person in this position gives up and may eventually end up in a mental institution.

If, on the other hand, the absence of stroking is combined with verbal abuse and/or physical brutalization, the child may move on into the next life position: I'M OK—YOU'RE NOT OK. This move comes from self-stroking. As the child is recovering from being beaten he learns to comfort (stroke) himself and thus concludes I'M OK by myself. A person who remains in this life position is not objective about his actions. He continually excuses himself and blames others. He says, "It is never my fault, always their fault." This position is occupied by incorrigible criminals.

The fourth and best life position, according to Harris, is I'M OK—YOU'RE OK. While the presence or absence of stroking determines the first three positions, the faculties of reason and choice determine the fourth position.[26] Harris compares choosing this new position to a conversion experience. The stated aim of Harris' book is "to establish that the only way people get well or become OK is to expose the childhood predicament underlying the first three positions and prove how current behavior perpetuates the positions." [27]

Harris and Freud

Harris uses the Freudian ploy of relating psychotherapy to medicine in order to give it credibility and make it acceptable. This might explain why he begins his book by first referring to Freud and then to neurosurgeon Penfield. In reference to Penfield's work, Harris says, "The evidence *seems* to indicate that everything which has been in our conscious awareness is recorded in detail and stored in the brain and is *capable* of being 'played back' in the present." [28] (Italics ours.) The word *seems* means "appears like" or "may possibly be" and the word *capable* means "can." However, Harris has concluded from Penfield's work that all of this material *is* stored in the brain and *does* determine our present behavior. He says, " . . . *our earliest experiences, though ineffable, are recorded and do replay in the present*." [29] (Italics his.) In addition, he contends that "the past invariably insinuates itself into our present life." [30] He calls this "the hook of the past." [31]

Even if it had been or could be proven that all of the experiences in our awareness are recorded in detail and remain in the brain, it is only a giant leap of faith that would cause us to conclude that they universally determine our behavior. It is not past experiences but present decisions that govern behavior. Because of Harris' psychiatric training, he is no doubt fixated on the past as a powerful determinant of present decisions and behavior and has merely redressed the Freudian fiction.

On the other hand, Harris does seem to hold an anti-Freudian position on free will, for he believes that a person can choose the fourth position, I'M OK—YOU'RE OK. He seems, on the surface at least, to have escaped Freud's unconscious determinants of behavior and preoccupation with the past. Nevertheless, he has not really escaped them; he has only limited their influence. According to Harris we are unconsciously determined by our early experiences to end up in the position of I'M NOT OK—YOU'RE OK. But he claims that this position is not permanent if one decides to change.

Harris contends that we can choose to be different, but that until we consciously decide to change we are conditioned and determined by our unconscious and our past history. In other words, we are not only determined to end up in one of the first three life positions, but our position established during childhood determines present behavior unless we decide to move into the fourth position. Excluding this decision to change, we end up with the same old Freudian determinism.

Harris has committed the further Freudian error of making I'M NOT OK—YOU'RE OK the universal neurosis of man. To support his position he quotes L. S. Kubie and adds his own italics:

> The clinical fact which is already evident is that once a central emotional position is established early in life, it becomes the affective position *to which that individual will tend to return automatically for the rest of his days*.[32]

Harris and Christianity

Harris stresses free will, responsibility and even morality. In fact, his book contains an entire chapter on his personal view of morality, in which he also presents his own personal view of Christianity. Because his view of Christianity sounds biblical, many Christians have erroneously accepted "the gospel according to Harris." Therefore, let us examine what he does say about Christianity to see if his ideas stand the test of Scripture, remembering that "all scripture is given by inspiration of God, and is profitable for doctrine, for reproof, for correction, for instruction in righteousness" (2 Tim. 3:16).

Sin

As we have already said, Harris claims that the universal condition of man is I'M NOT OK—YOU'RE OK. How the child arrives at this position underlies Harris' personal theology. Harris does not believe that a child is born into the condition of sin but rather that he chooses this position.[33] Thus, for Harris sin is a decision that a child makes about himself, rather than a condition in which a child finds himself. There is a subtle, but gigantic theological difference here. One idea is biblical; the other is not. The biblical position is that I'M NOT OK is the fallen nature of man, not a decision of man. We do not decide I'M NOT OK; it is our actual condition. "Wherefore, as by one man sin entered into the world . . . " (Rom. 5:12). "For as by one man's disobedience many were made sinners . . . " (Rom. 5:19).

According to the Bible, man does not arrive at the position I'M NOT OK; he is born into it. The reason man is NOT OK and feels NOT OK is because of his sin, not because of unconscious determinism or past history. NOT OK is just another name for the sinful condition of man as a result of the Fall. It is a condition for which there is only one cure and that is a right relationship with the Creator, *not* a theory and system of TA.

Born Again

As one can imagine, with a massive misconception of sin, Harris' resulting understanding of the born-again experience is also not biblical. Harris quotes Jesus' words, "Except a man be born again, he cannot see the kingdom of God," and then distorts the meaning. According to Harris, it is the civilizing process that forces a person into the position of sin, and one is born again by using his reason to understand his condition and to decide to change that position from one of I'M NOT OK to I'M OK.[34] Here again there is a subtle, but powerful, difference between deciding to make a change by virtue of the nature of human reason and choosing to accept what the Bible declares to be the source of new life.

According to Harris, one merely decides to be OK and he is. It is a natural, internal act. According to the Bible, one becomes OK as a result of deciding to accept what God has provided. It is a supernatural, external provision received within the very depths of man.

According to Harris, it is our action that makes us OK, but according to Scripture it is divine action. Harris' theory of OKness relies solely upon the work of man; the biblical truth is that it is the work of God. According to the Bible, I'M OK relies upon the provision of salvation and sanctification by the Creator, rather than upon a process of *self* transformation. The condition of sin is not erased or removed or changed by self; it is removed by God as one accepts the sacrifice Jesus provided for new life and as one accepts the power of the indwelling Holy Spirit to live the new life.

The peak experience of Transactional Analysis is I'M OK—YOU'RE OK, and the method of arrival is faith in self and in the TA system. However, the biblical truth is I'M NOT OK and YOU'RE NOT OK and never will be without a supernatural relationship with a supernatural God who sent His supernatural Son into this natural world to restore us to himself. No amount of theory or brilliance in writing will ever replace or erase this need from the heart of man. It is a need that most psychotherapists have never realized.

Transactional Analysis is a simple, easy-to-learn theory. It is high in simplicity but low in truth. It is low in truth about the condition of man and the means of change. Harris knows neither why man is NOT OK nor how he can become OK. The idea that I decide to be OK and then I am OK without repentance and forgiveness is both a new theology and a disguise for self-indulgence and self-centered love. It puts me at the center of both deciding to change and providing the means of change. It is, to use Harris' words, a system of "self stroking" par excellence.

Harris' new theology tranquilizes us to the truth about the condition of man and the process of change. He has replaced the biblical concept of the fallen condition of man and the provision for change with his own personal theology of unconscious determinism and self at the center of all things. Harris' theology is: I decide, I do, and I arrive.

One Way

The Bible declares very plainly that there is only one way of salvation: "Neither is there salvation in any other; for there is none other name under heaven given among men, whereby we must be saved" (Acts 4:12). According to the Bible there is only one way to God, and, as much as some may not like it, Christianity is in this sense an exclusivistic religion.

This exclusivism is a doctrinal absolute, and Harris declares, "There are no doctrinal absolutes." [35] Furthermore he contends:

> The truth is not something which has been brought to finality at an ecclesiastical summit meeting or bound in a black book. *The truth is a growing body of data of what we observe to be true.*[36] (Italics his.)

This is Harris' subtle way of saying that the basis for truth is not what is in the Bible, but rather what is in man. Truth according to Harris depends upon self and what self observes to be true. However, there are some things that are true, whether one observes them to be true or not.

Harris bases his ideas on the unproven theory of evolution and denies the claims of Christianity by saying that a small percent of the world's population could not possibly have exclusive truth. He quotes statistics on world population and the distribution of money, material possessions, food, life span, and religion. He contends that many more people know the name of Lenin than the name of Jesus and that the major communist documents outsell the Bible. He concludes by saying:

> We are deluded if we continue to make sweeping statements about God and about man without continually keeping before us the facts of life: the long history of the development of man, and the present-day diversity of human thought.[37]

What Harris is really saying is that considering our late

arrival in the so-called evolution of man and considering how we compare with the rest of the world materially, religiously, and numerically, how can we claim to have exclusive truth? What Harris may not realize is that *we* have not claimed exclusiveness; we have merely received it. It is not we who originally proclaimed it; the Scriptures have done so.

Opinions about evolution and the ideologies of the majority of the world have nothing to do with whether or not one has exclusive truth. Christians do not evaluate their view of God and the universe merely by present-day circumstances, the theory of evolution, or any other unproven theory of men.

> For what if some did not believe? Shall their unbelief make the faith of God without effect? God forbid: yea, let God be true, but every man a liar. (Rom. 3:3-4)

Grace

Besides rejecting the exclusiveness of Christianity and distorting the biblical concept of sin, Harris has also mutilated the biblical concept of grace. He has misshapen it to fit his own gospel of self-forgiveness and salvation through self. He says:

> The concept of grace . . . is a theological way of saying I'M OK—YOU'RE OK. It is not YOU CAN BE OK, IF or YOU WILL BE ACCEPTED, IF, but rather YOU ARE ACCEPTED, unconditionally.[38]

He quotes Paul Tillich's explanation of the incident in which a prostitute came to Jesus. Tillich says, "Jesus does not forgive the woman, but he declares that she *is* forgiven. . . . The woman came to Jesus because she was forgiven," and then Harris adds "not to be forgiven." [39]

At the end of this incident Jesus says, "Thy faith hath saved thee; go in peace" (Luke 7:50). Although she was accepted unconditionally, she received forgiveness and salvation through exercising faith. Acceptance and salvation are two different concepts. God loves and accepts every individual, and He has provided the means of forgiveness and salvation by faith. It is true that a person is accepted unconditionally, but it does not follow that a person receives forgiveness and is saved (from NOT OK to OK) unconditionally. Faith is necessary for receiving forgiveness and salvation. "For by grace are ye saved through faith" (Eph. 1:8). And this faith means faith in God, not faith in self or a system of TA. Harris is biblically wrong again. One does not become OK unconditionally; he must have faith in God.

In the same section of Scripture, right after Jesus says, "Thy sins are forgiven," it says, "And they that sat at meat with him began to say within themselves, 'Who is this that forgiveth sins also?' " (Luke 7:48, 49). Regardless of whether she was forgiven before or after she arrived, the important point is that forgiveness is necessary and that Jesus is the one who forgives, because of who He is. In a limited way, Harris examines what happened, but he does not think of who Jesus is. Harris has simply not gone far enough with the incident. The only one who has power to forgive sins is God himself. Jesus not only has the power to forgive sins, but has the authority to say, "Go and sin no more."

Harris further confuses the concept of grace by returning to his theme of the positions of man. He argues that a person's main problem is the NOT OK *position* of sin, not *acts* of sin, and that a person need only acknowledge or confess that he is in the wrong position to become OK. Such transition from NOT OK to OK is grace according to Harris. He further argues that confession of *acts* of sin is not only ineffective for change but that such confession cheapens the concept of grace and strengthens a NOT OK position.[40]

According to the Bible, our primary problem is *both* a position and an act. We were born in sin (position) and we do sin (act). 1 John 1:8 declares, "If we say that we have no sin, we deceive ourselves, and the truth is not in us." We do agree that if sin is a position only and not an act, then confession would be a waste of time. However, the Bible enjoins those who have been born again to "confess your faults one to another . . . " (James 5:16), and that "if we confess our sins, he is faithful and just to forgive us our sins, and to cleanse us from all unrighteousness" (1 John 1:9). According to the Bible it is necessary to recognize and confess both the position and the act of sin and to receive the forgiveness of God.

A New Gospel?

In the midst of writing his new gospel, Harris declares:

> If Transactional Analysis is a part of the truth which helps to liberate people, the churches should make it available. Many ministers who have been trained in Transactional Analysis agree and are conducting courses in Transactional Analysis for members of their churches as well as using it in pastoral counseling.[41]

TA is much loved in Christian circles, much taught in Christian colleges, and much practiced by Christian psychotherapists.

TA is accepted by many as truth because it sounds so close to the truth. Harris speaks of morality, sin, born again, and grace; however, Harris' concept of morality is not biblical, nor are his concepts of sin, born again, and grace. In Harris we have a gospel of universalism and a new path of salvation through mere self-forgiveness. About all Harris has done is to attempt to replace the fundamental truths of Scripture with a self-help game called Transactional Analysis. Upon close scrutiny and careful observation, one sees Harris with his TA game as just another angel of light.

26. The Whole Man

One major limitation to psychotherapy is that it rarely, if ever, deals with the spiritual aspect of man. Its main sphere of concentration is with the mind, will, and emotions. And even then, some forms of psychotherapy concentrate more heavily on the emotions than on the will and the mind, while other forms focus more on the intellect. Charles Tart tells us, "Orthodox, Western psychology has dealt very poorly with the spiritual side of man's nature, choosing either to ignore its existence or to label it pathological." [1] Sanctification, on the other hand, deals with the whole of man, which includes the body, soul, and spirit. Paul blesses his readers with these words:

> And the very God of peace sanctify you wholly; and I pray God your whole spirit and soul and body be preserved blameless unto the coming of our Lord Jesus Christ. (1 Thess. 5:23)

The only stream of psychotherapy which attempts to deal with the spiritual aspects of man is that which delves into the higher consciousness movement and other cultic and occult practices. Even though the fourth stream often involves the body, soul, and spirit, it offers merely a false means of sanctification or change.

The body, soul, and spirit are intimately related and interact with one another. However, according to the Christian position, the spirit has preeminence. It is through the spirit that we find the highest level of human existence. A nationally known nutritionist said something rather startling about this at the end of his lecture on nutrition. He said that if people had a choice between eating good food and not exercising or eating junk food and exercising, he would recommend the latter option. Of course he was not recommending junk food, but he was emphasizing the idea that exercise is even more valuable than good food.

He further pointed out that mental and spiritual health is even more important than exercise and good food. In fact, he said that if one had to make a choice, good mental and spiritual health should always be desired over exercise and good food, even though the latter are essential. His reasoning was that the mental and spiritual climate of a person will affect the bodily functions even more than good food and exercise.[2]

Many others agree that the spiritual aspect of man has an important effect on the total health of an individual. Paul Brenner, a medical doctor speaking to a community group, mentioned diet, exercise, and faith. He stressed that a person's belief system was the most important, with exercise taking second place and diet third.[3] He felt that the person's spiritual condition is far more important than what goes into his mouth. Jesus said:

> Do not ye understand, that whatsoever entereth in at the mouth goeth into the belly, and is cast out into the drought? But those things which proceed out of the mouth come forth from the heart; and they defile the man. (Matt. 15:17, 18)

The cornerstone of good total health is good spiritual health. A healthy physical life is related to a positive and stable mental-emotional life, which in turn is influenced by a sound spiritual life centered in Christ. Filling our stomachs with good food and flexing our bodies with good exercise contribute to health, but they are limited in their influence. Spiritual health is the most important and affects a person's entire life. The right spiritual condition is not only essential for eternity, but is vital for life right now.

Besides the spirit being the highest and most important aspect of man, the spirit is the deepest and most profound level of our being. Koestenbaum in *The New Image of the Person* tells how human needs are at a deeper level than that of most psychological theory. He believes that psychology deals inadequately with the hard questions about the meaning of life and existence. Such questions are of course in the spiritual realm.[4] The inner core of all non-organic mental-emotional problems is spiritual, not psychological. The cure is found in trusting and following the spiritual principles of the Bible, not the unproven theories and practices of psychotherapy.

Since most psychotherapeutic systems either reject or ignore the spiritual relationship between man and his creator, they deny the most vital aspect of man's nature. Psychotherapy is thus limited to those functions of a man which are totally unrelated to his basic life source. It is like treating symptoms without ever plumbing the depths of the inner man. Sanctification, on the other hand, deals with the whole man, through his spirit, which is the deepest and most significant element of his existence.

While on the one hand, psychotherapy may lead to symptom relief, it may, on the other hand, cover up a deep spiritual problem. Because psychotherapy rarely touches the spirit, it provides only superficial and limited relief. Psychotherapy may help a person to adjust, but it cannot transform him spiritually. A cry for help may actually be a cry for spiritual change. Psychotherapy is largely oblivious to such cries.

Sanctification, because it treats the whole man through his deepest and most profound area, his spirit, provides the means for a more significant walk in the supernatural realm, as well as for broader relief in the natural realm. Sanctification is a far more powerful force than psychotherapy in dealing with mental-emotional disorders. But, people have found that it is far easier to pay money for psychotherapy than to walk the much more difficult path of self-examination, discipline, and sanctification.

Spiritual solutions are not merely operative upon the spirit, for the Word of God applies to every aspect of daily life, including mental attitudes and interpersonal relationships. Besides the written Word, Christians have the Living Word, Jesus Christ. Jesus did not segment man; He saw each as an integral unit, but incomplete. He came to complete man, to fill the gap, to heal the past, to help in the present, and to provide hope for the future. He is still making men whole. The apostle John describes Jesus as "the light of men," the very source of life and love. Both the written Word and the Living Word minister to the whole man according to God's way, rather than according to man's feeble attempts.

The Old Nature and the New Nature

Christians are spiritual beings, new creatures in Christ. They are inherently different from nonbelievers as far as the new life within them. Because of this great difference they need to determine whether or not psychotherapy, as presented by the world, is God's way or man's way, whether it treats the old nature or the new nature. By comparing personality theories and psychotherapeutic systems and techniques with Scripture, they may discern whether such theories, systems, and techniques are of God, of man, or of Satan. "All scripture is given by inspiration of God, and is profitable for doctrine, for reproof, for correction, for instruction in righteousness: that the man of God may be perfect, thoroughly furnished unto all good works" (2 Tim. 3:16-17). Such examination is essential if a Christian is going to subject himself to such treatment or, moreover, if a Christian is going to use such ideologies and techniques to help other Christians.

Every aspect of a particular brand of psychotherapy must be checked with the following questions: Is this form of psychotherapy based upon ideologies which agree or disagree with Scripture? Or does this particular psychotherapeutic theory or technique merely reflect man's wisdom? "Beware lest any man spoil you through philosophy and vain deceit, after the tradition of men, after the rudiments of the world, and not after Christ" (Col. 2:8).

Since most personality theories and psychotherapeutic systems are based on a humanistic philosophy in which self is exalted and God is ignored or denied or distorted, these theories and systems are limited to dealing with what Scripture calls the "old man" or the "carnal nature." They attempt to fix up the unregenerate, non-Christian self and/or the Christian who is living by the self effort of his carnal nature.

God does not even try to fix up the old man. Instead, He counts the old man dead and buried and gives man a new nature which is spiritual and which is centered in Christ.

> Knowing this, that our old man is crucified with him, that the body of sin might be destroyed, that henceforth we should not serve sin. . . .
> Likewise, reckon ye also yourselves to be dead indeed unto sin, but alive unto God through Jesus Christ our Lord. (Rom. 6:6, 11)

The description of a Christian is thus:

> I am crucified with Christ: nevertheless I live; yet not I, but Christ liveth in me: and the life which I now live in the flesh I live by the faith of the Son of God, who loved me, and gave himself for me. (Gal. 2:20)

What psychotherapy attempts to heal, God has already pronounced dead, null, and void.

Psychotherapies are designed to help a person under the rulership of self (rather than under the rulership of Christ) so that he might better manage the difficult and impossible role of ruling himself and of meeting his own needs through self effort or manipulation of his environment. In the previous chapters we examined the various types of psychotherapy. The various psychotherapeutic approaches deal with the old nature, which might be called the old wineskin into which one cannot pour new wine, which is the new Christ life. Psychoanalysis and its many variations try to resolve conflicts of the old nature by returning to the past and discovering excuses for present behavior. The behaviorists attempt to show how the old nature can be changed by environmental controls (reward and punishment).

The many self theorists try to resolve present conflicts and anxieties by strengthening the self (the old man), by giving him a boost, by convincing him that all resources for improvement lie within him, by encouraging him to take a leap of faith into an I'M OK position, by removing dogma (including any authoritarian doctrine, such as the Bible), and by telling the self that he can choose and create his own standard and life.

The existentialists try to go beyond the old man, but in doing so, they awaken the spiritual nature with false gods and occult practices. Such forms of psychotherapy, because they are "spiritual," may not seem to elevate self, but in fact they delude self into thinking it can be higher and purer than anyone else and that self is indeed god.

The psychoanalytic and behavioristic systems make the therapist a god. The self theorists elevate the self as his own god. The existentialists provide a substitute god, which may be self, another person, an esoteric state of awareness, or an idol.

Although these various forms of psychotherapy may help a person deal with his needs and his problems, they are actually strengthening the old nature. By strengthening the old nature, they may actually be thwarting the possibilities for spiritual growth, since spiritual growth comes from reckoning the old man dead and learning to walk in the Spirit.

In contrast to psychotherapeutic counseling, true Christian spiritual counseling, which relies on Christ and is based upon the Word of God, is not meant merely to alter the behavior or change the attitudes of the old man. Instead, spiritual counseling attempts to establish the new man through salvation and ministers to the new man in the process of sanctification, which is the process of Christian maturity and becoming more like Christ. Without condemnation, a Christian spiritual counselor may lead a person from the old man into the new man according to the process described in Ephesians 4:22-24:

> You were taught, with regard to your former way of life, to put off your old self, which is being corrupted by its deceitful desires; to be made new in the attitude of your minds; and to put on the new self, created to be like God in true righteousness and holiness. (New International Version)

Psychotherapy only attempts to improve the old man and help him meet his own needs. In evaluating a psychotherapeutic system, a Christian would do well to see what aspects are for the old man or self and what can be applied to the new man in Christ. He should determine whether the system elevates God, self, or the therapist and whether it is God's way or man's attempt to alleviate mental-emotional suffering. Furthermore, he needs to be on guard for error that appears to be truth and for the subtle combination of man's wisdom and God's truth.

27. Faith, Hope, and Love

Although spiritual counseling promotes the sanctification and growth of the new nature in Christ and psychological counseling is limited to dealing with the natural, unregenerate man or the old nature, certain similarities and contrasts can be seen in the counseling process. Some of these similarities and contrasts lie in the realm of the interpersonal relationship between the counselor and the client. Traditionally, psychotherapists have claimed that their training, techniques, and theories are the most important aspects of the counseling situation.

Nevertheless, since no form of psychotherapy has proven itself to be clearly superior to other forms of psychotherapy, researchers are beginning to believe that the interpersonal relationship is the most essential ingredient for therapeutic change.[5]

> It should come as no surprise that helping people to deal with inner conflicts, to form viable relationships, to become less threatened and defensive, or to engage in more productive behaviors can be greatly facilitated in an interpersonal relationship that is characterized by trust, warmth, acceptance, and human wisdom. . . . This is not to say that techniques are irrelevant but that their power for change pales when compared with that of personal influence.[6]

We believe that faith, hope, and love are the main reasons why all psychotherapies have some degree of success. It is not a psychotherapeutic system that helps people; it is the psychotherapist himself who is able to love, stimulate faith and hope, and thus establish a relationship of confidence, trust, and growth.

Since the most effective basis for change lies in such universal virtues, they are not limited to the therapeutic setting.

Ministers, friends, and relatives can be at least as helpful to people suffering from mental anguish. Moreover, these interpersonal qualities are even more effective in spiritual counseling because they are not limited to natural faith, hope, and love, but involve the supernatural faith, hope, and love which originate with God and are expressed through His Word, His Holy Spirit, and His body of believers.

Faith and Hope

Besides attempting to alleviate mental-emotional suffering by only communicating with and analyzing the old nature, the practice of psychotherapy depends upon faith in the temporal rather than in the eternal. The Bible defines faith as "the substance of things hoped for, the evidence of things not seen" (Heb. 11:1). Thus, faith is belief in something or someone even though there is no conclusive, physical evidence that what is hoped for will come to pass.

A person may place his faith in himself, in another person, in ideas or abilities, in physical objects, or in what he hopes will happen. There is a great difference, however, between the world's view and practice of faith and hope and the biblical view. The faith and hope operative in the psychotherapeutic relationship are often misapplied and lack biblical direction, power, and fruit.

In the psychotherapeutic setting, faith ultimately rests in the therapist. A client hopes that the therapist will bring him healing, solutions to problems, and emotional well-being. Faith and hope rest in a man who is perhaps as vulnerable and weak as the client himself. Jerome Frank believes that the element of faith in the therapist accounts for the apparent success in psychotherapy. He says in his book *Persuasion and Healing*, "The essential ingredient of this relationship is that the patient has confidence in the therapist's competence and in his desire to be of help." [7]

Certain culturally established symbols are of importance in reinforcing the patient's faith and hope. The private office, secretary, framed degrees and licenses, and filled bookcases are all instrumental in raising expectations. People have learned to trust the individual in such an environment and to have faith in a system with these trappings.

Although it is indeed helpful to have faith and confidence in another person, a Christian's faith is to be centered in Christ. Throughout the Bible we are instructed not to trust in the wisdom of men. Paul was even concerned in his preaching: "That your faith should not stand in the wisdom of men, but in the power of God" (1 Cor. 2:5). Throughout the eleventh chapter of Hebrews, which is called the "faith chapter," every instance of faith is centered in the Lord: faith in the Lord's existence, character, and word. "But without faith it is impossible to please him: for he that cometh to God must believe that he is, and that he is a rewarder of them that diligently seek him" (Heb. 11:6). The Bible also says that faith and trust in the Lord lead to health:

> Trust in the Lord with all thine heart; and lean not unto thine own understanding.
>
> In all thy ways acknowledge him, and he shall direct thy paths.
>
> Be not wise in thine own eyes: fear the Lord, and depart from evil.
>
> It shall be health to thy navel, and marrow to thy bones. (Prov. 3:5-8)

Besides faith in the therapist, the practice of psychotherapy also depends upon a client's faith in the theory, system, techniques, and training of the psychotherapist. Thomas Szasz says, "Ritualized psychiatric interventions, I maintain, have no real therapeutic power, beyond that which the patient imputes to them." [8]

In the field of psychotherapy the psychotherapist and/or the particular brand of psychotherapy can act like a placebo. Arthur Shapiro, clinical professor of psychiatry at Mount Sinai School of Medicine, suggests that the power of psychotherapy may be merely the placebo effect. He says:

> Just as bloodletting was perhaps the massive placebo technique of the past, so psychoanalysis—and its dozens of psychotherapy offshoots—is the most used placebo of our time. [9]

Theory is not fact and treatment is not cure, but faith in

the system or psychotherapist does produce some results. Frank says, "This hope rests in part on the patient's faith in the therapist and the treatment method." [10] He says that experiments have confirmed "the hypothesis that part of the healing power of all forms of psychotherapy lies in their ability to mobilize the patient's hope of relief." [11]

A ludicrous example of how faith in a system can work is demonstrated in the use of a disposable guilt bag.[12] A kit of ten bags is sold to individuals who wish to deal with their guilt. Whenever a guilt bag user feels guilty, he pulls out a bag, takes a deep breath, and blows his guilt into the bag. Then he discards the bag. The success of this gimmick is directly related to a person's faith in it.

A friend of ours who is a professor at one of the California State Universities uses a method similar to the guilt bag. He has what he calls a "trouble box." Every time he wishes to dispatch burdens that get too heavy for him, he takes out his imaginary trouble box and puts each burden into the box.

The Christian, on the other hand, does not have to play games with himself. By faith he can receive forgiveness and healing from guilt. His faith rests in a living Lord and in the sure promises of God's Word. Rather than trusting in theory, he can know the truth and rely on the very source of truth. A Christian may need the help of another Christian in knowing and believing God's Word. He may need assistance in faith, but in the final analysis he looks to God to supply his deepest and most profound needs, as well as his daily and temporal necessities.

Faith, hope, expectation, and desire are strong elements in any situation and certainly in the therapeutic setting. Frank claims, "The apparent success of healing methods based on all sorts of ideologies and methods compels the conclusion that the healing power of faith resides in the patient's state of mind, not in the validity of its object." [13] Thomas Kiernan, author of *Shrinks, Etc.*, concludes his book by saying, "In the end, psychotherapy is a state of mind. If you are convinced it can help you, the likelihood is that it will; if you are convinced of the opposite, the likelihood is that it won't." [14]

If faith has that much power in itself, regardless of the object of the faith, think of how powerful faith is if it is truly directed towards God, and if the person exercising the faith is placing his faith in the God of the universe rather than in a mere man, and if he is placing his faith in the very Word of God rather than in a theory or system devised by man.

Like religion, psychotherapy is a method of faith healing. The faith one exercises influences his recovery. This faith can be exercised in a therapist or in the process of therapy. However, a higher octave of faith reaches up to the person of God and His process of help. One faith is in the natural and psychological; the other is in the supernatural and spiritual. Faith in the natural, though effective, is a lower order of faith than faith in the supernatural. Faith in the natural works because it is a step in the right direction, but faith in God is a greater step and is far more effective for healing the troubled soul. When this faith involves both the person of God and His process of cure, then peace, love, and joy will follow.

Love

An even more powerful factor than faith and hope is that of love, which is one of the central themes of the Bible. When Jesus was asked, "Which is the first commandment of all?" He answered, "The first of all the commandments is, Hear, O Israel; The Lord our God is one Lord: And thou shalt love the Lord thy God with all thy heart, and with all thy soul, and with all thy mind, and with all thy strength: this is the first commandment. And the second is like, namely this, Thou shalt love thy neighbour as thyself. There is none other commandment greater than these" (Mark 12:28-31). One of the most essential characteristics of God is love—so much so that the apostle John wrote, "God is love" (1 John 4:8). Therefore the most vital relationship for man, who was created in the image of God, is that of love—first a love relationship with God and second, a love relationship with other people.

The most common meaning of *love* is strong affection and concern for another person. We know from our own observation and experiences that love is most needed by babies and young children, but actually it is necessary for all of us throughout our entire life. One great tragedy is that most people have only a few love relationships and some people have none at all—none at work, none at church, and none even at home.

At the beginning of the psychotherapeutic movement and especially in the work of Freud, one of the cornerstones of psychotherapy was that the therapist's personality was to show as little as possible. The therapist was what is called a "transference figure." The patient was to transfer to the therapist attitudes toward important people in his past. The therapist could not be himself because he was required to represent those predominant figures in the patient's background. There are many therapists who still function in this manner.

However, now more therapists are meeting their patients as human beings, and more therapists are opening up and being friends with their patients. The major thesis of Paul Halmos' book *The Faith of the Counselors* is "that all forms of psychotherapy are based, not on a set of scientific facts or principles, but on an all-pervasive belief in the healing power of love." [15] Halmos believes that love is necessary for counseling to have a positive effect on a patient.[16] Szasz says, "Surely, works of piety and love, self-discipline and honest labor, are still infinitely better cures for what ails the human soul than medicines, mechanized psychotherapies, and mental health centers." [17] After about eight decades of psychotherapy we are back to Jesus' admonition to love.

Many people have said that all good therapy is simply a loving relationship. There is a great deal of truth to this. However, is it true that this love relationship actually exists in psychotherapy and, if so, to what extent? The answer to the first part of the question is obviously "yes." The answer to the second part is more complex. There are several things to be considered regarding a love relationship.

First, let us look at the idea of deep love as contrasted with superficial love. To deal with this issue, we need to understand first what love is not. Love is not a technique nor the result of training. We may be able to learn some external, observable gestures and expressions that may be interpreted as love. But, these are only outward manifestations. Some manifestations of love can be demonstrated by people who love very little.

Love is not a theory. There may be theories about love, but they do not fully explain what love is nor do they cause a person to be one whit more loving. Moreover, love is not solely an emotion. Many people love deeply at times without feeling great emotion. There is not just one word that adequately defines love, for love is an attitude, it is a commitment, it is an emotion and much more. The clearest demonstration of deep love was Jesus' act of sacrificial love when He died in the place of sinners and took upon himself the penalty for the sins of the world. Love puts high priority on the good of another person.

In relation to this sketchy description of love, let us look at the psychotherapeutic setting, which is a very special environment with built-in limitations. Furthermore, it is a uniquely artificial and contrived situation. Within this setting the therapist and the client meet for the client to gain emotional healing and for the therapist to provide what help he can in exchange for both immediate and far reaching remuneration and rewards. The relationship within the therapeutic setting differs from natural love relationships between persons. The differences can be seen in the following elements.

One to one. The first aspect is the one-to-one relationship in therapy. The main advantage is that the client has the therapist all to himself. But, it also has the disadvantage of excluding all others. On the one hand, the parenting and friending kind of relationships that therapists often provide can bloom in such a setting. But, on the other hand, this represents only one small facet of a deep, loving relationship, which may involve more than just a one-to-one interaction. Aside from group therapy, the psychotherapeutic relationship is almost exclusively one to one. While a one-to-one relationship is part of every love relationship, it is certainly not the whole of it.

A spiritual counselor, on the other hand, recognizes that a one-to-one relationship also is limited if it remains only on the human level, because without the love relationship with the Lord and the new life of the believer, the love is usually self-seeking or self-rewarding. The ideal situation for emotional healing is the flow of God's love into a person who is hurting from emotional distress. Such a flow may not come directly, but rather indirectly through another individual who is ministering God's love rather than his own. Additionally, a person who is suffering from mental-emotional problems needs to know and experience the love of God in his own being. Thus, the love is a circular love flowing through persons from God and returning to God.

One day a week. "See you once a week but never outside of the office if I can help it" is a definite limitation to a love relationship. Jay Haley points out the paradox of the therapeutic relationship. He says that while the relationship is "one of the most intimate in human life . . . the therapist . . . has no interest in seeing the patient outside the office." [18] Therapists generally avoid social contacts with their patients, and patients cannot see the therapist outside of this one day a week unless new appointments are made. Because of this limited one-day-a-week contact, the love relationship can definitely suffer, if it has been developed at all.

A spiritual counselor may meet with a person regularly to minister the love and truth of Christ. However, the relationship continues outside of a specific time which might be set aside. The church is beginning to realize the great importance of body ministry, of a caring and helping commitment of believer to believer. Jesus said that this love relationship between believers was the key to their identity as Christians (John 13:35).

One hour. In addition to limited weekly contact, the fifty-minute hour decreases the possibilities for meaningful, caring relationships. Why a fifty-minute hour? The fifty-minute hour is a device that meets the needs of the psychotherapist to regulate the flow of patients for the purpose of convenience and income. The length of time is not for the benefit of the counselee. Love relationships sometimes work on time schedules, but more often they do not.

The psychotherapeutic relationship is governed by the

clock, and if the client is late, he loses time from the already reduced hour. We can appreciate the positive aspects of a client meeting the time restraints of the system and we can understand that a therapist must see a number of patients throughout the day, but one must recognize that such restrictions do not lend themselves to developing loving relationships. The mark on the calendar and the hand on the clock must be followed, even if it means an interruption and "next please."

In a situation in which one Christian is ministering to another, time needs to be flexible. One does not turn on and off a relationship by the hand on the clock. Time is a precious commodity by which we can demonstrate our love for each other. Just giving time is a way of saying, "I care about you."

One fixed price. Besides one time per week and one fifty-minute hour, psychotherapy usually involves one fixed price. It is perfectly understandable that a professional person must be paid for his services. There's a need to pay the bills and to maintain an income. Nevertheless, the one fixed price does limit a love relationship; genuine love is not something one can buy. In fact, generosity is often an attitude that is expressed within a genuine friendship. The only possibility for such generosity within the psychotherapeutic relationship might be a discount for a long term or poor client. These, however, are the exceptions rather than the rule. Generally, if one cannot pay his bill, the relationship is terminated. The mark in the checkbook must match the mark on the calendar.

As with most professionals, time and money are two very important ingredients to a psychotherapist. In order to make a professional income, he must schedule and adhere to the fifty-minute hour. The fifty-minute hour regulates the number of patients per day, week, and month which, in turn, produce the necessary dollars per day, week and month. A psychotherapist must fill enough fifty-minute hours to make a desirable income. Thus, psychotherapy is a business that tends to revolve around time and money rather than around people and love.

Love is hardly a relationship which can be purchased with money. Jesus gave freely of His life and love and He asks us to do the same. "Love one another, as I have loved you" (John 15:12). A person who needs healing in the mental-emotional areas needs genuine love and friendship. The body of believers can and should offer this type of caring without basing the relationship on time and money. Christian spiritual counseling is a form of body ministry in which a love relationship is not based on the need to make an income; rather, it is a ministry which cannot be purchased with money.

One right after another. Since time and money are crucial to the professional psychotherapist, the regular process in a therapist's office is one person right after another, with patients going in and out of the office like factory workers on various shifts at an assembly plant. This is not a criticism of the treatment they receive once they arrive and have entered into their time slot. It is just a description of a process that works according to the clock. Patients know very well that they have been preceded by others and will be followed by more.

Time and money require numbers of patients. No one has set a limit on how many patients a day or week a therapist should ideally see. The American Medical Association estimates that the average psychiatrist has about 51 patient visits weekly.[19] One Christian psychotherapist brags about seeing forty-five people every week.[20] It seems that there is an assumption that numbers don't matter. The diminishing point of return is an individual affair; thus, no one sets a limit on numbers, and time and money become the final determinants.

Practicing therapy eight hours a day five days a week with large numbers of people always has and always will lead to superficial relationships lacking genuine love. It seems axiomatic that the greater the variety and numbers of people, the less effective we become. No amount of training, techniques, or licenses will overcome the obstacle of numbers.

Effective spiritual counseling cannot place itself in the trap of one-right-after-another. The spiritual counselor could hardly see numerous individuals because of the need to regularly intercede in prayer for each person to whom he ministers. Prayer between times of personal contact releases the power for change throughout the week. Since spiritual counselors depend upon God to do the real work of personal healing, they will desire to spend much time in prayer.

One Up; One Down

The therapeutic situation is filled with *one's*: a one-to-one relationship, one fifty-minute hour, one day a week, one fixed price and one right after another. The one's add up to one great advantage for the therapist but one great limitation for a real love relationship for the client. In true, natural, loving relationships persons are sometimes alone together and sometimes with others; they sometimes do things on a fixed schedule and sometimes spontaneously; sometimes one pays and sometimes the other pays. The things that happen naturally with close friends rarely or almost never happen in psychotherapy. Normally a rate is set and a service provided, but don't expect anything beyond what you paid for.

While it is true that therapists care for and love some of their patients, it is also true that they hate others, though the hatred is usually not intentional. Just as the personality characteristics of the therapist affect the patient, the patient's personality characteristics affect the therapist. Love is an important ingredient in the success of therapy, and the effect that the patient and therapist have upon one another in this area will increase or decrease the possibility of improvement for the patient. Add to this the lack of real involvement implied by the discovery of one researcher who "found that 50 percent of clinical psychologists no longer believed in what they were doing and wished they had chosen another profession." [21]

Because of all of the limitations we have just reviewed, the usual therapeutic situation provides little or no opportunity for the deeper aspects of healing love and friendship. A limited (one to one), timed (50 minutes), fixed (one day a week), paid ($25-75 per hour), routine (one right after another) relationship leaves little room for depth or creativity. Although an occasional relationship under these circumstances may have depth, most are generally superficial or absent of love. Nevertheless, some people are so hard up for love that even the most superficial looks good. Anything that looks even remotely close to the real thing will be gobbled up like a beggar taking crumbs. The patient often perceives any attention at all to be worthwhile and valuable.

It has been said that a psychotherapist is merely a paid friend, and a highly paid friend at that. Loneliness is a common affliction of Americans. The average person does not have a real friend and very few people in our society form real friendships. However, if someone doesn't have a friend he can rent one. And perhaps for some unfortunate people renting a friend is the only kind of friendship they can find. Psychotherapy at its best is rent-a-friend, but at its worst it's rent-a-service.

What a contrast between a paid friend and the kind of friendship which Jesus demonstrated. He said, "Greater love hath no man than this, that a man lay down his life for his friends" (John 15:13). Christians are called into a family love relationship: "Be kindly affectioned one to another with brotherly love" (Rom. 12:10). Thus, in ministering to the mental-emotional needs of other believers, a spiritual counselor would give his love freely. A true friend in Christ is of far greater value than a paid psychotherapist, not only because the love is freely given, but also because the source of the love is God.

Healing Virtues

There has been a great reluctance on the part of psychotherapists to recognize and accept the influence of faith, hope, and love, to practice these virtues, and especially to proclaim them as the healing virtues in psychotherapeutic relationships. One reason is that they are so enamored of the medical model of psychotherapy that the introduction of such ideas smacks of subjectivity and even sentimentality. In addition, each therapist, believing in his own brand of therapy, would like to think that what he is providing is related to his years of training rather than to the expectation of the patient.

To admit that improvement occurs because of faith, hope, and love, rather than because of psychotherapeutic training, techniques, and theories, would weaken the reason for fees. Finally, such virtues as faith, hope and love are the ones found in religion and faith healing. One who believes that he is a scientist, a professional practitioner, and a trained technician does not want to be considered a faith, hope, and love healer.

28. Spiritual Counseling

Because God created man to be a spiritual being in relationship to himself as well as a person with a mind, will, emotions, and body, there is a need for a counselor who can minister to the spiritual nature of Christians and who can bring nonbelievers into this new life of relationship with God. This kind of counselor has always existed in the body of Christ, but his ministry has been limited in much of the mental-emotional area of problems and disorders, because we have trusted what has claimed to be science more than we have trusted the promises of God.

The Bible speaks of such a spiritual counselor in Galatians 6:1-2: "Brethren, if a man be overtaken in a fault, ye which are spiritual, restore such an one in the spirit of meekness; considering thyself, lest thou also be tempted. Bear ye one another's burdens, and so fulfil the law of Christ." Thus, spiritual counselors are burden bearers with the ministry of restoration and sanctification or spiritual growth. They minister to the new man created in Christ Jesus, rather than to the old nature which has been counted null and void.

A Christian spiritual counselor is a minister or a lay person who centers his counseling in Jesus, who is the way, the truth, and the life. His main reference book is the Bible. Although a spiritual counselor may use observations about human behavior made by others, he tests each one with Scripture, because he believes that the Bible is the most accurate treatise on the human condition.

A true spiritual counselor does not place his confidence in any of the thousands of psychotherapeutic techniques, nor in the ideologies of determinism or humanism behind the personality theories. His confidence is in the truth as set forth in the Bible, the way of salvation and sanctification, which in-

cludes forgiveness, new life, walking in the Spirit, putting off
the old man and putting on the new. His confidence rests in
the very character and nature of the God of love. Rather than
relying on invented and learned techniques, he relies on the
Holy Spirit to minister through him according to God's wisdom, understanding, knowledge, compassion, forgiveness,
truth, nurture, guidance, comfort, strength, and very presence.

A Christian spiritual counselor's training and background
may vary, but his first prerequisite is that he has become a
child of God through the new birth spoken of in John 1:12-13:

> But as many as received him, to them gave he power to be-
> come the sons of God, even to them that believe on his name:

> Which were born, not of blood, nor of the will of the flesh, nor
> of the will of man, but of God.

Also, the Lord gifts certain believers for the ministry of
counseling so that not everyone in the body of Christ is per-
forming the same ministry.

> For as we have many members in one body, and all members
> have not the same office:

> So we, being many, are one body in Christ, and every one
> members one of another.

> Having then gifts differing according to the grace that is given
> to us, whether prophecy, let us prophesy according to the pro-
> portion of faith;

> Or ministry, let us wait on our ministering: or he that teach-
> eth, on teaching;

> Or he that exhorteth, on exhortation: he that giveth, let him
> do it with simplicity; he that ruleth, with diligence; he that
> sheweth mercy, with cheerfulness. (Rom. 12:4-8)

One whom God calls into spiritual counseling is gifted with
the ministry of exhortation balanced with the gifts of mercy
and teaching. He has a keen desire to help a person move towards the Lord, look to Him for guidance and strength, and
grow in faith. He encourages a person to walk in the Spirit and
to know God more intimately than before.

Although the spiritual counselor is gifted with the gift of
exhortation, he does not exhort in a negative sense, but rather

encourages a person by listening, caring, loving, and guiding. Because his main purpose is to encourage the growth of the new man in Christ, he himself has begun the spiritual walk of sanctification in that he recognizes the uselessness and negative pull of the old nature which God counts dead. He is a fellow struggler in life with the counselee, but he knows God and is walking after the Spirit. He himself knows the need to put off the old self, to be renewed in the spirit of the mind, and to put on the new nature which is in Christ. When he detects sin within himself, he confesses to the Lord and immediately receives forgiveness and cleansing. Thus, he shares his Christian walk with another person who has deep needs not only in the mental-emotional realm, but particularly in the spiritual realm.

The spiritual counselor becomes more like Christ through the process of sanctification. These qualities which are infused with the supernatural provide a fertile ground for distressed individuals to improve. The spiritual counselor encourages and instructs from Scripture and uses God's Word as the guide for life. He understands that man is a spiritual creation and ministers to this dimension of a person. He recognizes that the spirit of a man will influence and affect all of his life. Through gentle exhortation, nonpossessive warmth, loving mercy, and accurate teaching, a spiritual counselor may lead a distraught individual from darkness to light and from self-centeredness (which is a major cause of mental-emotional suffering) to God-centeredness, with God being the sole source of knowledge and understanding.

The spiritual counselor believes in his heart that God is faithful in all circumstances and that God allows circumstances, even adverse ones, for a person's growth. He trusts and teaches the truth of Romans 8:28.

> And we know that all things work together for good to them that love God, to them who are the called according to his purpose.

Thus, even though he may identify with compassion, he looks beyond the circumstances to the possible growth of the individual whom he is counseling. He will suggest ways to capitalize on circumstances, to benefit from pain and discomfort, to exercise faith, and to enter into Christ's victory in the midst of circumstances. As the spiritual counselor trusts God, he will be supportive of his counselee and will thus be a source of growth in faith.

Because much mental-emotional suffering and anguish come from either a misconception of the character of God or the misunderstanding of scripture, the spiritual counselor will spend time investigating the counselee's ideas of God and will share scripture as well as personal experience in order to help the counselee develop an accurate and healing conception of the character of God and His Word. He will emphasize such qualities of the Lord as love, compassion, power to help, forgiveness, mercy, and personal involvement. He will spend time helping the counselee come to know God personally and intimately.

Christians are called to minister to each other in the body of Christ. They are called to be a witness to a suffering and needy world. In order to minister to one another and to the world, Christians are given the gifts of ministry, which include spiritual counseling for mental-emotional unrest.

Training

One might wonder how a person can be a spiritual counselor if he is not trained in the same way as psychotherapists are trained. People feel nervous about trusting themselves to a person who is not trained in psychotherapeutic techniques. We have been taught to trust only the trained therapist. Yet, at the same time, the most powerful factors in a therapeutic setting cannot be taught: faith, hope, love, compassion, wisdom, listening, accepting, and understanding. Only ideas, theories, and techniques can be taught.

Even without the spiritual dimension of the Lord, researchers are beginning to reveal that psychotherapeutic training is not as useful as one might think. Jerome Frank has said, "Anyone with a modicum of human warmth, common sense, some sensitivity to human problems, and a desire to help can benefit many candidates for psychotherapy." [22]

A recent study of trained and untrained therapists by

Hans Strupp at Vanderbilt University compared the mental-emotional improvement of two groups of male college students. Two groups of "therapists" were set up to provide two groups of students with "therapy." The first group of therapists consisted of five psychiatrists and psychologists. "The five professional therapists participating in the study were selected on the basis of their reputation in the professional and academic community for clinical expertise. Their average length of experience was 23 years." [23] The second group of "therapists" consisted of seven college professors from a variety of fields, but without therapeutic training. Each untrained professor used his own personal manner of care, and each trained therapist used his own brand of therapy. The students seen by the professors showed as much improvement as those seen by the highly experienced and specially trained therapists.[24]

The question of dealing with extreme disorders has always been used by psychotherapists and others as the reason why lay persons should not counsel. The line of reasoning begins with the assumption that psychotherapy is effective with extreme disorders and that it is irresponsible to allow untrained people to deal with such problems. The next logical assumption is that if untrained lay persons cannot effectively deal with extreme disorders, they are no doubt ineffective with all mental-emotional problems.

However, the initial assumption of psychotherapeutic success with extreme disorders is now being severely criticized. The research mentioned in an earlier chapter pointed out that extreme disorders are now, more than ever before, considered to be biological in origin and that psychotherapy is *not* effective in such cases. Moreover, it has been discovered that psychotherapists generally do not even care to work with those who have extreme disorders.[25]

If psychotherapy is not effective with extreme disorders and therapists do not even care to work with those who have such disorders, then the important question is: who might be more effective with persons suffering from less extreme mental-emotional disorders? It seems with the results of research on trained and untrained "therapists" and with the relative success of all forms of psychotherapy that a modest conclusion would be that success is equally possible in either psychotherapy or lay counseling.

Techniques and training may give the therapist security and confidence, which in turn may increase his faith and hope, which then may affect the faith and hope of the patient. Training and techniques may thus influence the factors that directly affect the possibility for improvement. On the other hand, sometimes training and techniques blind a person to the truth. Training often gives one stereotyped ways of looking at human beings and can result in forcing a patient into a preconceived mold. Studies have indicated that patients often respond in ways that just happen to fit into the psychotherapist's training and background. Thus, the therapist's training and techniques may be limiting factors in the relationship, because they can condition the mind of the therapist and ultimately the mind of the patient. Techniques are often ways and even excuses not to get involved with patients. Many therapists consider that through these techniques they provide a service and that is what the patient is paying for.

Although a spiritual counselor is better off not having had exposure to psychotherapeutic theories and techniques, he requires a different kind of training. The Lord trains us first of all in the Christian walk and in ministering to one another. Furthermore, He has provided the greatest source book for spiritual counseling. Knowledge of the Word with an emphasis on scriptures which relate to the mental-emotional-behavioral realm is crucial. Additionally, it is helpful for those who are experienced in spiritual counseling to share from their own experience and knowledge.

As we become experienced in the things of God and see Him work in people's lives, we are more able to trust Him and we are more able to follow His leading in the counseling situation. We will see patterns emerge and become more adept at applying spiritual truth and scripture to everyday situations and to mental-emotional confusion.

Interpersonal Qualities

Hans Strupp has indicated that there are certain common ingredients in all psychotherapies that produce some success.[26] Jay Haley says, " . . . the exploration of the human psyche may be irrelevant to therapeutic change . . . it is argued here that change occurs as a product of the interpersonal context of that exploration rather than the self-awareness which is brought about in the patient." [27]

E. Fuller Torrey found that "the research shows that certain personal qualities of the therapist—accurate empathy, non-possessive warmth, and genuineness—are of crucial importance in producing effective psychotherapy." He concludes, " . . . therapists who possess these qualities consistently and convincingly get better therapeutic results than those who do not possess them." [28] Jerome Frank agrees that the "personal qualities of the therapist and the way he behaves soon outweigh symbols of his therapeutic role." [29]

It is our conviction that the interpersonal relationship in psychotherapy is a powerful ingredient for change, and, moreover, we believe that the interpersonal relationship within the body of Christ in the presence of God is an even more powerful force for true emotional healing and renewal. Institutional training and techniques do not necessarily lead to success in therapy. According to one researcher, "It has never been established that high levels of education and/or training are necessary to the development of an effective psychotherapist." [30] This same researcher says that while "warmth and empathy are highly important variables in determining client benefit . . . graduate programs do not help students to greatly increase their interpersonal skills." [31] The personal qualities of a counselor are far more important than his education. Torrey says, "There is strong evidence, both direct and indirect, upon which to build a case for . . . a person who is sanctioned . . . to do 'psychotherapy' even though he has not been so trained by acceptable Western professional standards." [32]

Because of the powerful effect of the personal qualities of the counselor and of the interpersonal relationship in the counseling setting, counselees are definitely influenced by their therapists, for better or for worse. The authors of *Psychotherapy for Better or Worse* note that "the therapist himself was one of the most often cited sources of negative effects in psychotherapy." [33]

Interpersonal qualities crucial to positive change in ther-

apy are life qualities, not trained techniques; they are char-
teristics of the individual, and in the Christian context they
are the characteristics of Christ himself, living and expressing
himself through the counselor. The secular psychotherapist
believes that it is his psychological background which causes
change. However, we contend that qualities such as faith,
hope, and love constitute the atmosphere for positive change.
To such interpersonal qualities, a spiritual counselor also depends upon the Word of God as he ministers to one with emotional needs.

Principles That Work

A number of the activities in spiritual counseling are similar to those in psychotherapy, but they do not originate with
psychotherapy, nor are they exclusive techniques of the psychotherapeutic world. In fact, three of them, which we will next
discuss, have existed ever since the Garden of Eden. They are
actually so simple and obvious that we often overlook them.
They are: listening/talking; confessing/accepting; and think-
ing/understanding. These activities of human interaction,
when intricately tied together and woven into the virtues of
faith, hope, and love, provide a powerful setting for growth
and improvement.

Listening/talking. Thomas Szasz has said, "There is no
such thing as psychotherapy. It is only a name we use for people speaking and listening to each other." [34] There is great
therapeutic value in the listening/talking relationship. However, listening is not a technique; it is a response of the entire
person. Although techniques of listening are actually taught,
such techniques are superficial. True listening is a heart response as well as a mental activity. Even though we can be
taught to pick up content of communication, the deeper understanding of a wise, compassionate listening response cannot be taught.

In most human settings hearing and speaking operate at a
very superficial level. Speaking is often used to give commands, to direct, to request, to explain, and so on. Nevertheless, a deeper talking/listening relationship is needed in life, in
which we can share ourselves with another person at the most

profound levels and communicate our dearest thoughts and loftiest dreams. Without the possibility of such person-to-person flow, internal stagnation can occur and emotional problems develop.

Love is also communicated through listening. In a spiritual counseling setting the listening/talking is not just limited to interaction between human persons. The Lord is also there listening, not only to the prayers and the sharing, but to the deep yearnings within a counselee's soul. Furthermore, the Lord may speak to the counselee or counselor through scripture or through spiritual intuition (the "still small voices").

Confessing/accepting. Another concept arises out of the listening/talking relationship, that of confession and acceptance. In a confession/acceptance atmosphere a person is free to bring up anything that is on his mind without fear of rejection. He might want to share a joyful thought or a nagging problem, but he has the freedom to share himself with another person.

There is real potential release in the freedom to confess and be accepted, and yet there are few relationships wherein we have such freedom to be ourselves. James encourages Christians to "confess your faults one to another, and pray one for another, that ye may be healed" (James 5:16). Paul warns against judging one another and advises, "Brethren, if a man be overtaken in a fault, ye which are spiritual, restore such an one in the spirit of meekness; considering thyself, lest thou also be tempted" (Gal. 6:1).

The freedom to be oneself can be compared to glass. Some glass is transparent through which we can see; other glass is opaque and only allows the passage of some light. We live most of life through varying degrees of opaqueness; but we thrive in the company of those with whom we can be transparent and freely allow our true selves to show. Many people live behind a facade in most of their daily situations, even in the marriage relationship and in the family.

Occasionally a ray of light escapes, but there are precious few moments when individuals feel completely safe and permit themselves to become transparent. In fact, these moments are so rare that few of us even recognize who we really are because we haven't allowed ourselves to be transparent. We haven't confessed ourselves to others or even to ourselves to get an accurate glimpse. To show our real self, we must know our real self; and to know our real self, we must show our real self. Knowing and showing our true selves are two sides of the same coin.

The principle involves more than just confession. It also involves acceptance. The two go together because confessing ourselves to others is enhanced when we perceive that another person hears what we have confessed and accepts us as we are. Confessing/accepting allows people to experience each other without fear of condemnation and to trust and feel safe in the presence of another. Notice how little we confess to people who condemn us. And unfortunately too many of our relationships are ones in which we confess ourselves very little because there is either limited acceptance or outright condemnation.

Lack of acceptance or outright rejection are common characteristics of our contemporary society. We all seem to envision ourselves as *self-styled critics*. Thus, more and more people show less and less of their real selves before others. And soon we know ourselves less because we have confessed ourselves less. The name for the final condition is *loss of identity*. And this is one reason why more and more people are seeking psychotherapeutic help. But, if we are aware of the healing power of confessing/accepting, we can apply it at work, at home, and in all of our relationships. We can provide the atmosphere for a confessing/accepting relationship with others and they with us.

Perhaps the most important aspect of confessing/accepting in the spiritual counseling setting is that of recognizing that the Lord accepts each person as he is, even though He may not condone the actions. The Lord accepts and loves the person and has provided the way of forgiveness so that as a person confesses his feelings, his hurts, and his sins, the Lord accepts him and forgives whatever needs to be forgiven. A spiritual counselor would thus want to reflect that same love and acceptance so that the counselee would feel free to confess and to receive forgiveness and cleansing rather than condemnation. Jesus did not come to condemn people, but to save them.

Thinking/understanding. Besides the listening/talking and confessing/accepting relationships, one more vital principle emerges. This principle could be called thinking/understanding or wisdom. As one person shares himself with another in a loving, accepting atmosphere and grows through the confessing/accepting process, he becomes wiser in his thought life.

Just as we have lost contact with our real selves by not confessing ourselves and not exposing the real self, so too have we lost touch with our own thought processes. We have been so regimented by a generation of True-False and Multiple Choice tests and by the rise of mass computerization, that we tend to operate with restricted, rigid, computer-like thinking. However, we cannot relate the computer-like test answers to life problems.

We have sadly failed to place high value on thinking and understanding; furthermore, we know so little about it that the whole subject frightens us. We tend to like to stay with the safe, the right and wrong answers, the things we can measure, and the things we can quantify. Thus wisdom and understanding take a back seat to thinking that is more commonly acceptable, more measurable, and more akin to the computer.

Mental-emotional problems fall outside the grip of the computer. The computer soon runs out of capacity for such complex problems and we are left on our own. The computer was invented and developed to solve human problems, but the problems computers solve are problems of speed and quantity, not feeling and emotion. The problems of feeling and emotion can be solved only by the person himself. We can provide an environment for thinking, understanding, wisdom and truth, but the solution must be discovered by the person himself. And he must use the kind of thinking that we are not trained to do and often avoid at all costs.

Thinking/understanding in the spiritual setting is again not limited by human abilities or human wisdom. The Bible says that Christians have an extra dimension of spiritual discernment. In fact Paul exclaims that "we have the mind of Christ" (1 Cor. 2:16). Thus we are not limited to intellectual insight; instead we can have spiritual insight. The Lord created the complex human mind and He is able to bring clarity out of confusion and truth out of error. He promises to give us wisdom as we ask for it, and He gives us revelation concerning His involvement in our situations. Paul prayed for the Ephesians:

> That the God of our Lord Jesus Christ, the Father of glory, may give unto you the spirit of wisdom and revelation in the knowledge of him:

> The eyes of your understanding being enlightened; that ye may know what is the hope of his calling, and what the riches of the glory of his inheritance in the saints. (Eph. 1:17-18)

While all of these processes of listening/talking, confessing/accepting, and thinking/understanding may occur in psychotherapy, they are limited in such a setting because they are used for other purposes than for a person to come into a deeper and fuller walk with God. Also, such activities, though beneficial in themselves, can lead persons into error if they are used by persons whose ideologies and theologies are not in agreement with the Bible. Such activities in merely a secular situation are limited to the natural, carnal man and may, thus, not touch the spiritual aspects of a person.

Instruction in God's Word and experience in the areas of listening/talking, confessing/accepting, and thinking/understanding will enhance the abilities of a spiritual counselor. The Lord supernaturally gifts certain people along these lines, and a spiritual counselor would then use these gifts to edify or build up a person's faith and spiritual walk.

Spiritual Values

Training in the Word of God is essential for a spiritual counselor because counseling involves a value system as well as interpersonal qualities. The Christian value system includes a biblical pattern for living as well as moral standards.

The value system of Scripture is far superior to those of man-made philosophies. The closer the biblical pattern is followed, the greater the possibility for both spiritual growth and improvement in the mental-emotional realm. Some psychotherapies include a value system with some similar principles, such as responsibility and self-restraint. However, the Christian does not need to look to the ways of man when God has already given us a path to follow and a plan to use.

All forms of psychotherapy expose a person to a value system and each psychotherapist will either alter it to fit his own values or adjust his own value system to agree with that of a particular psychotherapy. A psychotherapist attempts to change a person's value system as well as his actions. Hans Strupp maintains that for therapy to be effective the patient must give up his past philosophy of life and adopt a new one. He says that both a new value system and practical lessons in constructive living are essential for therapeutic success.[35]

The crucial question, then, for the Christian is: To what value system am I subjecting myself—that which comes from the Bible, that which originates with men, or an amalgamation of the two? Quite often a person evaluates a psychotherapeutic value system on a subjective level rather than measuring it objectively with Scripture. Frances Roberts in her devotional *On the Highroad of Surrender* writes:

> It is not in the heart of a man to discern his own way. Much that is evil man calls good, and much that is good men curse because a man will bless what he enjoys and condemn what gives him displeasure.[36]

The value system in the Bible may involve self-sacrifice, pain, and relinquishment. However, by following the teachings of Scripture one finds truth and gains true freedom (John 8:31, 32, 36).

We cannot escape the question of morality when we are dealing with values. Thomas Szasz declares:

> Human behavior is fundamentally moral behavior. Attempts to describe and alter such behavior without, at the same time, coming to grips with the issue of ethical values are therefore doomed to failure.[37]

Although some psychotherapists are beginning to understand the importance of morality, few will accept biblical standards of morality as the basis for human behavior and as an antidote for human anxiety.

To most psychotherapists the word *sin* is taboo. They do not want to label sin *sin* for fear of being judgmental, moralistic, and harsh. Nevertheless, some are beginning to realize the basic problem of sin. Karl Menninger in his book *Whatever Became of Sin?* defines sin as "transgression of the law of God; disobedience of the divine will; moral failure." [38] Throughout his book he shows that mental health and moral health are identical. In the book *The Seven Deadly Sins Today*, Henry Fairlie contends that it is necessary to live by moral standards in our words and actions in order to experience satisfactory and positive living. He believes that "if we do not take seriously our capacity for evil, we are unable to take seriously our capacity for good. The understanding that we sin is a summons to life." [39]

The major thesis of Donald Campbell's presidential address to the American Psychological Association was that modern psychology is more hostile to religious morality than is scientifically justified.[40] He mentioned that "many aspects of human nature need to be curbed" but that "psychology and psychiatry, on the other hand, not only describe man as selfishly motivated, but implicitly or explicitly teach that he ought to be so." [41] He declared, "It is certainly my impression, after 40 years of reading psychology, that psychologists almost invariably side with self-gratification over traditional restraint." [42]

He felt that the assumption of traditional psychotherapy—that a person should not have to repress or inhibit his biological impulses and drives—"may now be regarded as scientifically wrong." [43] Campbell further declared, "I am indeed asserting a social functionality and psychological validity to the concepts of sin and temptation and of original sin due to human carnal, animal nature." [44]

Christianity provides man with both a personal God and a personal morality. God has declared, from the very beginning, the importance of moral standards in the life of man and has consistently called man to a virtuous life. Belief in the personal God of the Bible and the application of His moral system are beneficial to mental-emotional health. The Scripture declares, "For God hath not given us the spirit of fear; but of power, and of love, and of a sound mind" (2 Tim. 1:7). God and His moral law are inseparable. When man questions

God's moral system, he questions God. Conversely, when he questions God, he questions God's moral system. On the other hand, there are great mental and physical benefits from following God and His law.

Sin and morality are not only involved in developing mental-emotional disorders; they are also involved in the way to mental-emotional restoration as sin is confessed and new ways of behaving are adopted. Violation of God's laws lead to poor mental health, but sound morality leads to a sound mind. Any system of treatment or help must take this into consideration.

Szasz says with respect to treatment, " . . . psychotherapeutic interventions are not medical but moral in character." [45] Watson and Morse say, "Thus values and moral judgments will always play a role in therapy, no matter how much the therapist attempts to push them to the background." [46] Therefore, a counselor's values and moral beliefs are important to consider since his own beliefs will influence the values and moral behavior of his client. The spiritual counselor uses biblical standards for behavior, biblical doctrines to help man, and biblical revelations to learn the true nature of man.

Although moral standards may vary from person to person and from culture to culture, man is by nature a moral being. Many problems in adjustment to life's demands and opportunities are related to this moral nature. Much mental anguish arises from a distorted sense of morality and from both true and false guilt.

Because the vast variety of moral standards within the psychotherapeutic framework originate from human conceptions and misconceptions of morality and because psychotherapeutic systems do not recognize the scriptural standards of morality nor the biblical means of relieving guilt, psychotherapy is not able to deal adequately with either morality or guilt. Nor is it able to guide a person into a biblically sound, virtuous life.

Psychotherapists often attempt to free clients from morality systems by changing the standards to fit the person. In doing so they are actually creating other morality systems, less restrictive perhaps, but nevertheless systems which deal with morals and values. Both spiritual counselors and psychotherapists work to change attitudes, values, and behavior, and yet they are quite different. Spiritual counseling uses the Bible as a touchstone and focuses on the legitimate spiritual nature of man. Psychotherapies, on the other hand, have relative, changing, and unreliable morality and value systems and basically disregard the spiritual core of man. Spiritual counseling promotes biblical morality and standards of behavior and deals with the crucial factors of sin and guilt.

The perfect value system lies within the Word of God. And along with His value system, God has supplied the Holy Spirit to enable the Christian to live by biblical standards and the blood of Jesus to take away sin and guilt. Jesus came to give new life to believers so that they could be rescued from the bondage of sin and guilt and so that they can live the new life according to the instructions and power that He gives.

Besides a righteous value system, the Bible contains practical instructions for changing attitudes, thoughts, and behavior through a renewing of the mind (Rom. 12) and through walking in the Spirit (Rom. 8). Such changes lead to love, joy, peace, and other positive characteristics, as well as to a deeper love relationship with the Creator.

Reprise

Although both the psychological way and the spiritual way claim to lead a person to mental-emotional stability and positive changes in thought and behavior patterns, they are actually quite different. The psychological way originates with man, utilizes man-made techniques, and ends with man. The spiritual way originates with God, employs gifts and fruits of the Spirit, and leads a man to a greater awareness of God and of himself as created by God. The psychological way is based on man-made philosophies, mainly humanism, but the spiritual way is based upon biblical principles.

The psychological way is a combination of techniques and theories, but the spiritual way is a synthesis of love and truth. Jesus said, "I am the way, the truth, and the life" (John 14:6), and the apostle John defined God as "love" (1 John 4:8). The psychological way involves changing standards and flexible morals. The spiritual way follows the unchanging standard and authority of the Word of God.

The psychological way has self at the center, while the spiritual way is centered in Christ. The psychological way mainly attempts to treat the mind and emotions of a man apart from his body and his spirit. The spiritual way considers the whole man and brings healing to the mind, the emotions, the will, and the body through bringing them into a balanced relationship to the spirit and thus to God himself. The psychological way attempts to change a man's thinking and behavior through the mind, will, and emotions. The spiritual way changes a person's thinking, emotions, and behavior through his spirit.

The church would do well to develop this ministry so that it might provide for the deeper needs of individuals, so that it might minister personally to those people who are suffering from mental-emotional stress, that it might minister to those people who are facing difficult situations and changes in their lives, so that it might even minister to those who are suffering from deep emotional disorders. Only a spiritual counselor can minister to the spiritual nature of man.

Part Seven

Broken Cisterns and Living Waters

29. Rejection of the Living Waters

In the past, religion and science were the main ways of achieving our aspirations. More recently, to the consternation of some and the satisfaction of others, the license for ensuring our well-being has apparently been transferred to psychotherapy![1]

Psychotherapy from its very beginning created doubt about Christianity. Each in his own way, the two great men of psychotherapy, Sigmund Freud and Carl Jung, eroded confidence in Christianity and established negative ideas concerning Christianity that prevail today. Freud (1856-1939) was a Jew, and Jung (1875-1961) was a Protestant. Both of these men influenced the faith and affected the attitudes of many people concerning Christianity and the role of the church in the healing of troubled souls.

Freud believed that religious doctrines are all illusions and that religion is "the universal obsessional neurosis of humanity."[2] Jung, on the other hand, viewed all religions as collective mythologies, not real in essence, but real in their effect on the human personality. For Freud religion was the source of mental problems, and for Jung religion, though merely a myth, was a solution to mental-emotional problems. Thomas Szasz states, "Thus, in Jung's view religions are indispensable spiritual supports, whereas in Freud's they are illusory crutches." [3]

As the views of these two men influenced our culture, many Christians began to doubt the effectiveness of the Bible and the church in dealing with life problems. On the one hand, if one is religious he must be sick; and on the other hand, religion is merely a necessary fantasy. While Freud argued that religions are delusionary and therefore evil, Jung contended that all religions are imaginary but good. Both positions are anti-Christian; one denies Christianity and the other mythologizes it.

How did Freud and Jung come to such conclusions about religion? According to Atwood and Tomkins, " . . . all theories of personality will remain colored by subjective and personal influences." [4] According to Szasz, "The popular image of Freud as an enlightened, emancipated, irreligious person who, with the aid of psychoanalysis, 'discovered' that religion is a mental illness is pure fiction." [5]

Szasz contends, "One of Freud's most powerful motives in life was the desire to inflict vengeance on Christianity for its traditional anti-Semitism." [6] He also shows how Freud made his hostility towards religion look like an objective conclusion from the realm of science. He says, "There is, in short, nothing scientific about Freud's hostility to established religion, though he tries hard to pretend that there is." [7] Freud was surely not an objective observer of religion. According to Szasz, he was a man who incorporated his personal feelings towards Christians into a supposed scientific theory about all religion.

While Freud grew up in a Jewish home, Jung was raised in a Christian home and his father was a minister. He wrote of his early experience with the Holy Communion, which seems to be related to his later ideas about religions being only myths. He says:

Slowly I came to understand that this communion had been a fatal experience for me. It had proved hollow; more than that, it had proved to be a total loss. I knew that I would never again be able to participate in this ceremony. "Why, that is not religion at all," I thought. "It is an absence of God; the church is a place I should not go to. It is not life which is there, but death." [8]

Because of Jung's essential misunderstanding and misconceptions, Christianity, the church, and Holy Communion seemed hollow and dead.

From this one significant incident, Jung could have proceeded to deny all religions as Freud did, but he did not. He evidently saw that religion was very meaningful to many people. Thus, he accepted them all, but only as myths. His choice to consider all religions as myths was further influenced by his view of psychoanalysis. According to Viktor Von Weizsaecker, "C. G. Jung was the first to understand that psychoanalysis belonged in the sphere of religion." [9] Since for Jung psychoanalysis itself was a form of religion, he could hardly reject all religions without rejecting psychoanalysis.

Freud and Jung each turned his own experience into a new belief system called psychoanalysis. Freud attempted to destroy the spirituality of man by identifying religion as an illusion and calling it a neurosis. Jung attempted to debase the spirituality of man by presenting all religion as mythology and fantasy. Contemporary psychotherapists have not moved very far from these two positions. They continue to present religion as an illness at worst and as a myth at best.

Freud and Jung had enthusiastic followers who helped promote their ideas. Furthermore, the media assisted by giving uncritical publicity to the psychoanalytic movement with books, movies, and TV romanticizing this mania. The academic world furthered the cause of psychotherapeutic thinking by failing to identify the shortcomings of the new cult. Even medicine promoted psychiatry by incorporating it as a medical specialty. And worst of all, church leaders helped to propagate the theories of Freud and Jung by embracing the ideas they liked and ignoring the rest, not discerning the anti-Christian cancer which would eat away at the very soul of the church.

Abandoning trust in God, both Freud and Jung led their followers in the quest to find answers to the problems of life within the limited ideas and standards of men. They developed a philosophy, a psychology, and a psychotherapy of self-deification. In the psychoanalytic, humanistic and existential streams, actions, words, and thoughts are inevitably directed inward. In the psychoanalytic stream, the unconscious and its pathways through free association and dreams constitute the doctrine of this faith. In the humanistic stream, the self and its pathway of direct experience and feeling are the substance of salvation. In the existential stream, the self is still glorified, but to a higher level of exaltation with so-called higher consciousness as its supreme goal.

Because they rest on different foundations, move in contrasting directions, and rely on opposing belief systems, psychotherapy and Christianity are not now, nor were they ever, natural companions in the healing of troubled souls. The "faith once delivered unto the saints" was displaced by a substitute faith, often disguised as medicine or science, but based upon a foundation of humanism which is in direct contradiction to the teachings of the Bible. In considering the relationship between psychotherapy and religion, Jacob Needleman observes:

> Modern psychiatry arose out of the vision that man must change himself and not depend for help upon an imaginary God. Over half a century ago, mainly through the insights of Freud and through the energies of those he influenced, the human psyche was wrested from the faltering hands of organized religion and was situated in the world of nature as a subject for scientific study.[10]

From its very beginning, psychotherapy was developed as an alternate means of healing, *not* as an addition or complement to Christianity or to any other religion. Psychotherapy is not only offered as an alternate or substitute method of healing troubled souls, but also as a surrogate religion.

Arthur Burton says, "Psychotherapy . . . promises salvation in this life in the same way that theology promises it in the afterlife." [11] In speaking of what psychotherapy has done to religion, Szasz contends, " . . . contrition, confession, prayer, faith, inner resolution, and countless other elements are expropriated and renamed as psychotherapy; whereas certain observances, rituals, taboos, and other elements of religion are demeaned and destroyed as the symptoms of neurotic or psychotic illnesses." [12]

In referring to the displacement of the spiritual with the psychological, Szasz says:

> Educated in the classics, Freud and the early Freudians re-molded these images into, and renamed them as, medical diseases and treatments. This metamorphosis has been widely acclaimed in the modern world as an epoch-making scientific discovery. Alas, it is, in fact, only the clever and cynical destruction of the spirituality of man, and its replacement by a positivistic "science of the mind." [13]

It is not only a matter of the destruction of the spirituality of man" but a destruction of religion itself. Szasz further contends:

> . . . medical psychiatry is not merely indifferent to religion, it is implacably hostile to it. Herein lies one of the supreme ironies of modern psychotherapy: it is not merely a religion that pretends to be a science, it is actually a fake religion that seeks to destroy true religion.[14]

He warns about "the "implacable resolve of psychotherapy to rob religion of as much as it can, and to destroy what it cannot." [15]

A current answer given by a psychiatrist to the question of whether there is conflict or compatibility between religion and psychotherapy is this:

> Psychiatry has a quarrel with only those forms of religion which emphasize the doctrine of original sin. Any belief that tends to focus on the idea that man is inherently evil conflicts with the basically humanistic approach to problems that psychiatrists must follow.[16]

God's view of man according to the Bible is not compatible with the psychoanalytic view of man. Nor is the biblical condition of man accepted or promoted by any of the many brands of psychotherapy.

Psychotherapy has attempted to destroy religion where it can and to compromise where it cannot. A supernatural void has been left as a result, and the need to believe in something has been filled by making a religion out of the ritual of psychotherapy. Psychotherapy has debased and virtually replaced the church's ministry to troubled individuals. During this time the priests and ministers have been devaluated and have been intimidated into referring their parishioners to the new psychotherapeutic priests. The people no longer look to the pastors and ministers for such help nor do they look to the Bible for spiritual solutions to mental-emotional problems.

Szasz tells us that "the psychiatrist displaces the priest as the physician of the soul." [17] The psychotherapists have not only displaced the priests and ministers, but have themselves become god figures. One book refers to "the 'Jehovah effect,' in which the therapist recreates patients into his own image." [18] In fact, this same book reveals that those patients who become more like their therapists are rated as most improved by their therapists. The psychotherapist has attained the level of adoration, mystery, and divine regard once accorded to the clergy. He has even become the object of worship because he is supposed to have all the answers and understand all the mental mysteries of life.

Now the cycle of deception is complete. The psychotherapist offers man a new, less demanding, less disciplined, more self-centered substitute for religion, for that is what psychotherapy is; a new false solution to mental-emotional problems, for that is what the psychological way is; and a new god figure, for that is what the psychotherapist has become. Now people flock to this surrogate religion with its unproven ideas and abstract solutions. They flock to the new high priest and worship at strange altars. People have fallen for the false image of the psychotherapist priest and for the theology of therapy.

Cure of Souls or Cure of Minds?

From the very beginning of the Christian church there was a method and a ministry for dealing with mental-emotional problems. The method depended upon the Word of God, which describes both the condition of man and the process of relief for troubled minds. The ministry was a prayer and healing ministry which dealt with all nonorganic mental-emotional disturbances. This entire process was known as the "cure of souls." John T. McNeill in *A History of the Cure of Souls* describes this ministry as "the sustaining and curative treatment of persons in those matters that reach beyond the requirements of the animal life." [19]

One aspect in the process of the cure of souls dealt with sin as a basis for mental-emotional problems and included forgiveness with healing through repentance and confession. This practice was later formalized and became one of the sacraments of the Catholic church. The Sacrament of Penance, which includes repentance, confession and forgiveness, has been one of the most important functions of the Catholic church.

James, the head of the first Christian church in Jerusalem, exhorted, "Confess your faults one to another, and pray one for another, that ye may be healed" (James 5:16). Confession was used in the early church as a means of both forgiveness *and* healing. The biblical doctrine of confession and forgiveness was a means of mental-emotional healing from the very inception of the church and actually dated way back to the early days recorded in Genesis. In the twelfth century confession and absolution became one of the Catholic sacraments, but this merely formalized a practice which already existed.

Martin Luther opposed the system of indulgences in the church, but he strongly supported the practice of confession. He wrote, "Of private confession I am heartily in favor. . . . It is a cure without an equal for distressed consciences." [20] He further declared, "I would let no man take confession away from me, and I would not give it up for all the treasures of the world, since I know what comfort and strength it has given me." [21]

The biblical pattern of confession for mental-emotional healing remained an important part of the church until the rise of psychotherapy. As well as continuing through the Catholic practice of confession, the cure of souls was a vital aspect of early Lutheranism and remained an important function throughout the entire Protestant movement until the church relinquished this ministry to psychotherapy.

One might argue that while confession has dramatically diminished in the Protestant church, it still exists in the Catholic church. A close examination of the Sacrament of Penance, however, will show that though the sacrament still exists and has even become more diversified in recent years, the attitude about its use has changed considerably through the influence of psychotherapy. At one time the act of confession not only led to forgiveness for the sins of the penitent, but also the priest ministered to the emotional damage which had resulted from the sin. Although the liturgy and ritual of confession still exist, little ministry is provided in the sacrament for mental-emotional hurts.

The attitude towards the sacrament, the role of the priest, and the relationship between priest and parishioner have all radically changed since the rise of psychotherapy. The shift has occurred from one priestly role to another, from a priest who had both a sacramental role in the administration of this rite and a pastoral role in dealing with mental-emotional problems (resulting from sin) to a priest who has merely a sacramental role. The priest has been persuaded to give up his role as counselor and to refer those who have mental-emotional disorders to trained and licensed professional psychotherapists. Priests and ministers have been convinced that they do not have the knowledge or ability to deal with such problems. In some cases priests and ministers have received training in psychotherapy and use some of these techniques and devices to replace their previous reliance on Scripture and their former confidence in ministering to the mental-emotional results of sin.

There is an exception to this pattern, however. Those individuals who are less educated and are in the lower socio-economic classes continue to seek counsel from their priests. Because poor and uneducated people seem to have escaped the psychopropaganda, they still use the priest as pastor and counselor in the problems and distresses of life. On the other hand, people who are affluent and educated not only seek out the psychotherapist, but are readily referred by the priest who voluntarily has abdicated his pastoral role.

The priest has relinquished and the psychotherapist has usurped the pastoral role, and both priest and parishioner know it. The professional psychotherapist is the new priest, and a secular rite of psychotherapy replaces the sacred rite of confession. Church people now exhibit more faith in the secular confessional known as psychotherapy than in the sacred confessional known as Penance. The pastoral role has been downgraded and the psychotherapeutic role has been elevated, but psychotherapy has operated as a sterile substitute for the healing balm of confession.

The cure of souls is not solely limited to Penance. The cure of souls includes all aspects of spiritual activities that treat the realm of nonorganic mental-emotional problems. It also involves an inward change through repentance from sin, which results in a change of mind and heart and of thought and behavior.

The cure of souls, which once was a vital ministry of the church, has been displaced by a cure of minds (psychotherapy). The switch from spiritual healing to psychological healing was made subtly and secretly. It began in the secular world and then like a little leaven it infiltrated and infected the whole church.

Within the church (both Protestant and Catholic) a transition occurred in which people who were suspicious and skeptical of conservative Christianity and who lacked knowledge of and experience with the deeper spiritual life accepted a new message. And that new message was a psychological message about man, devoid of the basic biblical principles and, in certain instances, sprinkled with just enough biblical words to make it sound Christian. Many in the church were ignorant of the real meaning of this new message and accepted the new faith in psychotherapy. As a result, a psychology of self became the norm, faith in self became the creed, and the fundamental and eternal truths were laid aside.

Mistakes of the Past

Some of the blame belongs to the church. At one extreme there was too much emphasis on outer ritual rather than on inner change. At the other extreme there was an overemphasis on demonism as the only cause of emotional problems. Historically we have seen the disastrous results of man's attempts to deal with emotionally disturbed persons. Without scriptural basis but in the name of Christianity, the church tried to treat insanity by some of the most inhumane methods of physically imprisoning, torturing, and punishing. The church also took on the attitude of the Pharisees and adopted the technique of exhortation through condemnation. Thinking that identifying the sin would lead to repentance and change, they forgot to use the methods of compassion, understanding, and love exemplified by Jesus.

Because man's attempts were combined with certain doctrines of Christianity and perpetrated by the church, the world has pointed an accusing finger at the church in the area of mental-emotional problems. The world has seen only the errors and evils of an ignorant section of the church which actually was *not* following God's way of healing as set forth in the Bible. Thus, the world and psychotherapists particularly have claimed to be more humane and compassionate. However, when we look at the present horrors of involuntary incarceration of the insane, electroshock therapy, frontal lobotomy, the side effects of thorazine and other drug therapies, the sexual exploitation of women by certain therapists,[22] and the noxious effects of some of the psychotherapeutic techniques, we might ask, "Which are more cruel?"

Because of mistakes of the past, the church has adopted a tenuous position. It dares not take a firm stand in the area of the cure of souls because of the accusation that the church, in the past, has equated mental-emotional disorders with demonism. The spectre that hangs over the church is the memory of witch trials and witch burnings. But these were mistakes of men in the church; they were not errors in God's Word.

To its credit the church does not want to be in the witch burning business anymore and it does not want to carry on inquisitions. However, in a desire to avoid one extreme error, it has committed another. It has, in this instance, given up the need for inquiry in its attempt to avoid inquisition. Thus, the church has avoided investigation into the value of psychotherapy and has blindly accepted and adopted its theories and practices. At the same time it has abandoned one of its most vital responsibilities to its members by giving up on the cure of souls ministry as if it were a giant mistake in church history.

Another fear of the church is that of acting unscientific, for the Copernican spectre echoes its hollow laugh at the early church fathers who believed that the earth was the fixed center of the universe. This spectre causes the church to be fearful of making an error which science will later reveal. Just as the church erroneously hung onto the Ptolemaic model of the universe and was wrong, it is fearful now of rejecting the so-called scientific and medical model of the cure of minds. Thus, in attempting to avoid error, the church has given up the true for the false.

At the same time, with the rise of science and technology, the church has become more materialistic and less interested in the spiritual aspects of life. As psychotherapy became attached to science and medicine, it became attractive to the church as a seemingly legitimate means of relieving the disturbed soul. As a result, more and more people sought answers to their problems outside of the church.

Sin or Sickness?

Whereas once the church believed in, spoke of, and practiced the cure of souls, it has shifted its faith to a secular cure of minds. Szasz very ably describes how this change came about: " . . . with the soul securely displaced by the mind and the mind securely subsumed as a function of the brain—people speak of the 'cure of minds.' " [23] The brain is a physical organ; the mind is not. With this subtle semantic twist, the mind (disguised as an organ of the body) was elevated as a scientific and medical concept in contrast to the soul, which is a theological idea. A choice was made between a so-called scientific concept and a theological one. The average person does not see that both mind and soul are abstract concepts. One is an abstraction of psychotherapy and the other is an abstraction of religion.

At the same time that a physical organ (the brain) was replaced by an abstraction (the mind), another change took place. Whereas the church had believed that there was a relationship of sin and circumstances to mental-emotional disorders, the psychotherapist introduced the medical concept of sickness to explain such disorders. Nevertheless, mental suffering is not synonymous with sickness. We have only been deluded into thinking that it is. We easily accepted the word *sickness* to refer to mental-emotional problems because that was the "loving" and "understanding" way to cover up moral responsibility—ours as well as theirs.

One of the main purposes of Thomas Szasz in writing *The Myth of Psychotherapy* was this:

> I shall try to show how, with the decline of religion and the growth of science in the eighteenth century, the cure of (sinful) souls, which had been an integral part of the Christian religions, was recast as the cure of (sick) minds, and became an integral part of medical science.[24]

The words *sinful* and *sick* in parentheses are his. These two words mark the dramatic shift from the cure of souls to the cure of minds.

There is a serious problem when people confuse passion with tissue and sin with sickness. Such confusion of words leads to erroneous thinking. And this very confusion and error virtually ended the cure of souls ministry in the church. Through a semantic trick, the mind was confused with the brain and the misnomer of sickness replaced the concept of sin. And the entire subjective, theoretical process of psychotherapy ensconced itself safely in the realm of science and medicine. But, in reality, psychotherapy is a misfit as medicine and an impostor as science.

The recipe was simple. Replace the cure of souls with the cure of minds by confusing an abstraction (mind) with a biological organ (brain), and thus convince people that mental healing and medical healing are the same. Stir in a dash of theory disguised as fact. Call it all science and put it into medicine and the rest is history. With the rise in psychotherapy, there was a decline in the pastoral cure of souls until it is now almost nonexistent. Secular psychotherapy has taken over to such an extent that Szasz says, "Actually, psychotherapy is a modern, scientific-sounding name for what used to be called the 'cure of souls.' " [25] Thus we have the shell, without the power, without the life, and without the Lord.

Accepting the Living Waters

Christianity is more than a belief system or a theological

creed. Christianity is not just what happens one hour a week in church. Christianity is faith in a living Lord and in His indwelling Holy Spirit. Christianity involves the entire life: every day, every action, every decision, every thought, every emotion. One cannot adequately treat an individual apart from this life force. Nor can we segment the mental and emotional from the belief system of a person. For too long we have looked to the church to answer our theological questions and we have looked elsewhere for answers to our life problems. Christians who have God's Holy Spirit living in them are spiritual beings; therefore they need spiritual solutions, not merely psychological attempts.

It is understandable that the world would reject the Living Water in seeking to understand and help individuals suffering from mental-emotional problems. However, as the world rejected the biblical answers, the church began to doubt its own doctrine of sin, salvation, and sanctification in the area of mental-emotional disorders. Many ministers even left their pastorates to become licensed psychotherapists.

In the past eighty years psychotherapy has displaced the soul of man with the mind and has replaced the cure of souls with the cure of minds. The psychological has usurped the place of the spiritual, and even Christians look to psychotherapy rather than to sanctification as a means of dealing with soul problems. It is our position that the Bible provides both a spiritual basis for mental-emotional health and a spiritual solution for nonorganically caused mental-emotional disorders. True mental health involves spiritual and moral health as well as emotional well-being. It is time for Christians to take a fresh look at the Bible and at the provisions which God has available for mental-emotional health and healing.

30. Diluted, Polluted, or Pure?

The biblical basis and spiritual solutions are all that are necessary for establishing and maintaining mental-emotional health and dealing with nonorganic mental-emotional conditions. There is no need for both spiritual and psychological solutions. There is no need to add psychotherapy to spiritual counseling which leads to sanctification. We need simply and solely to rely on the spiritual and return the ministry of the cure of souls to its proper place in the church. In a discussion with the governor of California, Thomas Szasz very clearly recommended that the responsibility for mental health care should be taken away from the professions and given to voluntary associations such as churches. He declared, "I would turn this whole business back to the ministers and priests and rabbis." [26]

One very difficult task, however, will be convincing Christians that there are not two equally good ways to solve mental-emotional problems, the spiritual way and the psychological way. An even more difficult task will be convincing Christians that a so-called blending of the psychological and the spiritual only emasculates Christianity because of the inherent conflicting belief systems of the two. There is only one way for Christian believers and that is the spiritual way, the biblical way.

We hope that we have revealed throughout this book enough misconceptions, misunderstandings, and mistakes about psychotherapy to enable the reader to at least question whether the psychotherapeutic way is a valid means of dealing with mental-emotional disorders.

The so-called virtues of the psychological way are mostly based upon self-serving testimonials and opinion rather than upon research and fact. Each generation since the advent of psychotherapy has brought forth its psychotherapeutic innovators who have insisted upon the success of their systems. Jerome Frank says, "A historical overview of Western psychotherapy reveals that the dominant psychotherapeutic approach of an era reflects contemporary cultural attitudes and values." [27] In contrast to this we know that the Bible contains eternal truths about man and his condition. We know that the biblical doctrines and principles are beneficial as a healing balm for men. God's Word does not change with the culture and the times.

The available evidence should discourage anyone's preference for psychotherapy over spiritual counseling. The spiritual way always has been and continues to be the proper and successful way to deal with mental-emotional problems. Even if the spiritual way did not exist, the psychological way is questionable at best and detrimental at worst. We are not attacking the psychological way merely as a means of establishing the spiritual way. The psychological way is suspect no matter what one might say about the spiritual way.

The church does not need psychotherapy and its convoluted systems of loose theories and fabrications offered as facts. Psychotherapy, from its very beginning, has been and still is detrimental to Christianity. It has dishonestly usurped the ministry of the cure of souls and it distorts any form of Christianity to which it attaches itself.

Amalgamation

In spite of the fact that historically and philosophically many aspects of psychotherapy have been directly or indirectly antagonistic to Christianity, many people believe that the two are complementary, that psychotherapy and Christianity are perfectly compatible as used simultaneously or separately under different circumstances.

The church has fastened its faith on psychotherapy and believes its claims beyond proof or justification. At the same time, the church has become suspicious and doubtful of the validity of spiritual solutions to mental-emotional disorders. Thus the element of the self-fulfilling prophecy has transpired here. People have been rewarded according to their expectations. When one believes in psychotherapy and doubts religion, it is no wonder that the psychological way looks so good and seems successful and the spiritual way appears inadequate. It has all happened according to man's faith.

One of the largest referral systems to psychotherapy is the church. Christians are quite regularly referred to psychotherapists by unsuspecting priests and ministers who have been convinced that they are not able to help such people and that only the professional has the expertise required for counseling an emotionally disturbed person. The referral occurs not only because the clergy and the church have been talked out of the cure of souls ministry, but because the pastor does not really have the time to deal with such persons.

In most cases, ministers and priests are referring their people to a system that they know little about but have been convinced to accept as valid. Most pastors could not defend this system except by drudging up the defunct medical model or by leaning upon some unsupportable generalizations about the supposed effectiveness of psychotherapy. Most ministers could not even tell you the predominant psychotherapeutic orientation or the success or failure rate of the therapist to whom he sends his flock.

Many Christians have either questioned or left "the faith once delivered unto the saints" to follow after one or more of the 200 psychotherapeutic myths. Through the guile of psychotherapy and the naivete of the church, the holiness of Christianity has been exchanged for the hollowness of psychotherapy. And many have made the transaction as if it were all done for scientific and medical reasons. The fact is that they have exhibited a faith in the psychological which has exceeded their faith in the spiritual, and they have done it all for less than objective reasons.

One Christian psychotherapist wrote, "I am convinced, however, that the psychoanalytic method in the diagnosis of human behavior is a valid one." [28] A Christian psychiatrist tells in his book about the wonderful advantages of psychiatry and particularly of Christian psychiatry.[29] A well-known Southern California minister read about the four basic temperaments of Hippocrates and proclaims them with a spiritual message even though the theory behind them has never been shown to be valid.[30]

Christian seminaries now train ministers as clinical psychologists and counselors, and many Christian colleges offer the services of psychiatrists, clinical psychologists, psychiatric social workers, and counselors to minister to the mental-emotional needs of all. Psychotherapy is so universally acclaimed and believed in and accepted in the Christian world that one would think the church had received it as a vision from on high.

Many Christians believe that psychotherapy provides real truths about man and can be trusted to help improve human behavior. The question is: which truth is true truth? There is not one Christian psychotherapeutic way. Christian psychotherapists follow a variety of the over 200 schools of thought available. Psychotherapy, both outside and inside of Christianity, provides a diversity of methods and belief systems. There is much the same confusion and contradiction of psychotherapeutic thought both in and out of Christianity. We know that the spiritual principles in the Bible are eternal, but which psychotherapeutic principles are eternal? The Psalmist wrote, "The Lord bringeth the counsel of the heathen to nought: he maketh the devices of the people of none effect. The counsel of the Lord standeth forever, the thoughts of his heart to all generations" (Ps. 33:10-11).

The Christian psychotherapist believes in combining both the spiritual way and the psychological way. His faith is in a recipe that adds the ingredients from both. However, does he study psychotherapy to find an elaboration of spiritual truths or as an end in itself? For example, the Bible distinctly teaches that man has a free will and is normally responsible for his behavior. Does the Christian psychotherapist look to psychotherapy to state such a truth or to elaborate upon it? Does the Christian psychotherapist place the Bible or psychotherapy first? Does he think first of the spiritual or of the psychological?

Although the intent of the Christian psychotherapist may be to place Scripture first, does he convey this idea to his counselee so that they both know that the Word of God is preeminent in all things? Or, do those who come to the Christian psychotherapist merely learn to trust psychotherapy more? Put simply, do people have a greater confidence in Scripture or in psychotherapy after seeing the Christian counselor? How many times has a Christian psychotherapist knowingly or unknowingly exalted a psychotherapeutic idea over a biblical doctrine? How often has a psychotherapeutic idea influenced belief in a biblical doctrine when it should have been the other way around?

Even if the Christian psychotherapist places the Bible first, there is a danger, after having once found a biblical truth in psychotherapy, of adopting other ideas that may be contrary to Scripture. How much psychotherapeutic garbage has the Christian psychotherapist taken in and dispensed as a result of accepting therapeutic systems which *sound* like biblical ideas? Although the combination of Scripture and psychotherapy may begin compatibly enough, there is no telling where it will end. Psychotherapeutic techniques and theories should not be inflicted upon spiritual principles, nor should the Bible be forced to fit psychotherapy. True spiritual counseling should come out of biblical principles.

It may be that some Christian psychotherapists' hidden reason for the lack of complete dependence upon Scripture is that this position might raise the whole question of charging fees for services. If the Bible is sufficient and counseling is a ministry of the church, what is the rationalization for charging a fee? If one can maintain the bankrupt medical model and defend professional training in psychotherapeutic techniques, charging a fee is perfectly justifiable.

The popularity and proliferation of psychotherapy in Christian circles have given it a validity and visibility that it does not deserve. As we have indicated in the beginning of this book, there are still questions about whether or not psychotherapy even works, how it works, and on whom it might work. As we mentioned earlier, psychotherapy is a system filled with many unproven theories and few facts. It is a ridiculous delusion to go on believing in the romance and ritual of psychotherapy. It is a field that is filled with speculative and spurious thought, which sometimes ends up killing one's confidence, confession, and convictions in Christianity.

The psychotherapeutic system usually centers on self and appeals to a sick and sinful society. We have for too long been seduced by this orientation of self-centeredness which produces only a pseudosolution for the soul. The safest and sanest thing for Christians to do is to replace psychotherapy with spiritual counseling in the church. Such a reversal would be a welcome relief from the woes of a system that is so subjective and so incapable of providing objective proof or validity. Reestablishing the spiritual counseling ministry and abandoning the psychotherapeutic domain would no doubt prove illuminating to the entire church.

It is the Scripture, not psychotherapy, which reveals the

true condition and nature of man. The Bible contains sufficient information and counsel for maintaining mental-emotional health and for ministering to mental-emotional problems. There may be psychotherapeutic systems that will help man to feel better or to indulge himself without feeling guilty, but none of them has any eternal value.

Psychotherapy is the counterfeit currency of the world and a substitute for the healing balm of Gilead. And Christian psychotherapy is a house divided against itself. How long shall we have one foot in the wilderness of the cure of minds and one in the promised land of the cure of souls?

Faith in What?

In all honesty, there is no conclusive evidence or final proof for either the psychological way or the spiritual way. It is our faith that has led us in one direction or the other. No one has proven outside of faith the superiority of either way. When a person chooses one way over the other, it merely constitutes a leap of faith in one direction or the other. Most psychotherapeutic concepts hover in the realm of the mystical and even the theological. Psychotherapy is swathed in theories which are believed as fact *by an act of faith*. It is dishonest not to admit the element of faith and to insist that psychological theories are universal facts. Such theories rest on the same need for faith as religion does. They are wholly dependent upon faith.

Some might argue that certain testimonials support the use of the psychological way and others the use of the spiritual way. But, when we overlook the testimonials in either direction and look at all the hard evidence, the conclusion is that neither the psychological way nor the spiritual way has final proof of either superiority or greater effectiveness of one over the other. Each requires faith. The question is, are we going to place our faith and trust in the systems devised by men or are we going to believe and trust God's Word as set forth in the Bible?

The psychological model has not proven itself as a substitute for the spiritual model either theoretically or practically.

The cure of minds malfunctioned from the very beginning and has floundered ever since. If psychoanalysis had done what it pretended to do, men would never have had to invent over 200 other therapies and thousands of techniques to do the job. The fact that so many different therapeutic systems are currently being tried indicates that not much is really known about the cause and cure of mental-emotional disorders. Proposed causes and attempted cures are merely guesses as to how to deal with such problems.

Psychotherapy has proven to be like the naked monarch in the fable "The Emperor's New Clothes." For almost eighty years it has proliferated itself and permeated our society. It has captured the hearts and minds of the people and turned the head of the church away from the cure of souls. Like the emperor, psychotherapy stands proud and tall in its supposedly beautiful garments and few have dared whisper, "The emperor has no clothes!" The emperor is naked and few have the vision or courage to speak up and say so. Few dare speak out because neither society nor the church wants to be part of an inquisition. Furthermore, the church is self-conscious about its recurring image of appearing narrow-minded. And so, all stand and look at the emperor and pretend that he is wearing fine apparel.

People have pretended so long and so hard that they actually believe he has on the most elegant clothes ever created. Because they have been fearful of the possibility of repeating the error of the inquisition, they have accepted an illusion. Unfortunately, many people both in and out of the church do not want to deal with the facts of his nakedness and would rather believe a delusion and live in ignorance.

The Supernatural Quest

There is no question that the main-line psychotherapies will lose their power over the populace. They will diminish for some of the same reasons that the church lost its power in the personal lives of believers in the realm of mental-emotional problems. Since the church tended to relate these disorders to disobedience or demonism, cures were directed against sin or

Satan. (While it is true that everything wrong in the world is due to sin, there are sins within us, those inflicted upon us, and those that exist in this decaying world.) The church overlooked circumstances and organic illness as possible causes and, thus, through simplicity lost respect. Psychotherapy, on the other hand, has overlooked the most vital and most complex aspect of man, his spirit.

Psychotherapy as we now know it has failed and will fail because it is filled with a simplicity that defies both proof and denial. The possibilities of demons and disobedience have been replaced by symbols and sickness. At the present state of knowledge no one can prove the final cause of disorders of the mind. Psychotherapists can only puff themselves up, use the best rhetoric they can muster up, and hope that someone will line up behind them.

Man cannot escape his need for the supernatural. He can distort it; he can attempt to substitute it; he can deny it; but he cannot escape it. The cosmic loneliness we find in literature, the reaching outward for union with the seemingly unknown, and the seeking inward to find meaning in life are all indications of the desire to unite with the supernatural.

This is the first century in the West during which many do not have a basic realization of salvation or an understanding of the meaning of life. Thus, people are looking to psychotherapy, astrology, biorhythms, ESP, and even UFO's and extraterrestrial beings to fill the void. They are looking for an easy psychological salvation that does not recognize the fallen condition of man and an easier psychological sanctification which does not involve the spiritual process of growth. The jacket cover of Christopher Lasch's book *The Culture of Narcissism* states:

> The narcissistic personality of our time, liberated from the superstitions of the past, embraces new cults, only to discover that emancipation from ancient taboos brings neither sexual nor spiritual peace.[31]

We predict that to fill this spiritual void and escape the growing criticism of main-line psychotherapy, new forms of psychotherapy which follow the religious nature of man will become increasingly popular. They will discard their scientific sheep's clothing and blatantly turn to the occult. They will expand their interest in higher consciousness to include a mish mash of Eastern and Western religions. They will combine elements of psychotherapy and religion with all kinds of occult beliefs and practices.

Already a new form of psychotherapy has arisen on the scene, which mixes the Freudian search into the past with reincarnation. The jacket cover of *Past Lives Therapy* by Morris Netherton says, "A renowned psychologist shows how your present problems and anxieties are the result of what has happened to you in your past incarnations, stretching back centuries." [32] The book claims cures for colds, migraine headaches, stuttering, and so on. Such combinations of psychotherapeutic theories and techniques, religious beliefs and practices, and the occult will have vast appeal to the numerous people disillusioned with the old-time psychotherapy and desiring to fill the vacuum left by the absence of true biblical faith.

The first indication we had of this was several years ago when a clinical psychologist told us that the new psychotherapy would join psychological principles with occult principles in order to minister to people. He is a licensed psychotherapist and uses psychology together with astrology in his practice. At that time it seemed like an incredible idea; now it's obvious.

The Bible warns about combining humanism with the occult.

> For thou hast trusted in thy wickedness: thou hast said, None seeth me. Thy wisdom and thy knowledge, it hath perverted thee; and thou hast said in thine heart, I am, and none else beside me.

> Thou art wearied in the multitude of thy counsels. Let now the astrologers, the stargazers, the monthly prognosticators, stand up, and save thee from these things that shall come upon thee. (Isa. 47:10, 13)

Ancient Babylon was condemned because its religion deified self and embraced the occult. The future Babylon, spoken of in the book of Revelation, is a revival of a combination of humanism, self-glorification, false religions, and the occult.

Many aspects of psychotherapy, and especially the fourth

stream, fit right into the biblical description of Babylon. Needleman reports:

> A large and growing number of psychiatrists are now convinced that the Eastern religions offer an understanding of the mind far more complete than anything yet envisaged by Western science. At the same time, the leaders of the new religions themselves—the numerous gurus and spiritual teachers now in the West—are reformulating and adapting the traditional systems according to the language and atmosphere of modern psychology.[33]

Ralph Metzner, a clinical psychologist, in his book *Maps of Consciousness* explains how the I Ching, Tantra, Tarot, alchemy, astrology, and Actualism work and claims that these occult practices can be used to achieve meaning in life and can lead to mental-emotional growth and health.[34]

In his book *From Shaman to Psychotherapist*, Walter Bromberg says that there are at least 250 mystical methods for attaining a higher consciousness. He observes:

> Whereas in previous generations "altered consciousness" was considered a mark of bohemian depravity if sought voluntarily or one of madness if involuntary, nowadays a "high" is the essence of psychologic sophistication. The procedures for attaining greater awareness of the sensory world within, or to put it bluntly a "good feeling," vary tremendously.[35]

And we might add that the possible combinations of the 250 mystical methods and the thousands of psychological techniques stagger the mind.

Jesus, on the other hand, advised:

> Enter ye in at the straight gate: for wide is the gate, and broad is the way, that leadeth to destruction, and many there be which go in thereat:

> Because strait is the gate, and narrow is the way, which leadeth unto life, and few there be that find it. (Matt. 7:13, 14)

Living Waters

Psychotherapy has tried to maim the hand that holds the sword of the spirit and has made the church vulnerable in soul ministry by providing all sorts of substitute psychological ideas in place of genuine spiritual solutions. Psychotherapy even offers all kinds of trinitarian psychotherapeutic models to draw people away from the Father, Son, and Holy Spirit.

God spoke through the prophet Jeremiah and said:

> Hath a nation changed their gods, which are yet no gods? but my people have changed their glory for that which doth not profit.

> Be astonished, O ye heavens, at this, and be horribly afraid, be ye very desolate, saith the Lord.

> For my people have committed two evils; they have forsaken me the fountain of living waters, and hewed them out cisterns, broken cisterns, that can hold no water. (Jer. 2:11-13)

The psychological way is a broken cistern while the spiritual way is the Living Water. The psychotherapists have filled their broken cisterns with the water from the four polluted streams of psychology.

The church has waited too long, has drifted too far, and has largely given up the Living Waters for broken cisterns in the area of mental-emotional healing. The church has drunk this polluted water and poisoned its soul ministry until it is nearly nonexistent. And, in its attempts to replace this needed ministry, the church has turned to the world of psychotherapy in search of the ministry which was destroyed by psychotherapy.

The church not only permitted the cure of minds to replace the cure of souls ministry without substantiation or proof, but has embraced psychotherapeutic theories, techniques, terminology, and theology in its blind desire to meet the needs of a suffering generation.

All mental-emotional problems that have no organic base can be best ministered unto by the Word of God. God has asked in His Word, "Whom shall I send, and who will go for us?" (Isa. 6:8). This is a call to serve and to minister. We have a choice to make based upon faith, because there is no final proof for either the psychological way or the spiritual way. How long shall we "halt between two opinions"?

Some Christians already believe in and preach the use of the cure of souls rather than the cure of minds. Paul Billheimer in his book *Don't Waste Your Sorrows* says, "Except where there is organic difficulty, the root of all conflicts in the home is not mental but spiritual. Psychology and psychiatry are usually totally irrelevant." [36] Clinical psychologist Lawrence Crabb says in his article "Moving the Couch into the Church":

> Counseling therefore belongs ideally in the local church and not in the private professional office. . . . I don't consider private counseling *wrong*. I rather see it as less than the best, something that exists and will probably continue to exist because churches are generally not doing a very good job.[37] (Italics his.)

We have a living God, the source of all life and healing. We have His living Word. His Word contains the balm of Gilead for the troubled soul. His Word ministers healing to the mind, the will, and the emotions. Ray Stedman in his book *Folk Psalms of Faith* refers to all the written revelation of God as "the law of the Lord." He quotes Psalm 19 which says, "The law of the Lord is perfect," and then he declares:

> It is complete, there is nothing left out. It is comprehensive, it does everything that we need it to do. There is no part of your life, no problem that you will ever face in your life, no question with which you will ever be troubled, that the Word of God does not speak to and illuminate and meet.[38]

We believe that the Lord fully intends to restore the ministry of the cure of souls to the church. He will use both ministers and lay believers who will stand on the completeness of the Word of God. They will minister under the anointing of God's Holy Spirit and rely on God's principles outlined in His Word. They will operate as a priesthood of all believers and minister God's love, God's grace, God's mercy, God's faithfulness, and God's wisdom to those who are suffering from mental-emotional hurts and problems. They will voluntarily give of their time, their love, and their prayers to lift the heavy burdens. They will fulfill Paul's admonition:

> Brethren, if a man be overtaken in a fault, ye which are spiritual, restore such an one in the spirit of meekness; considering thyself, lest thou also be tempted.

> Bear one another's burdens, and so fulfill the law of Christ. (Gal. 6:1-2)

The Lord has indeed promised more to His church than a

Dead Sea. He has promised Living Water!

> In the last day, that great day of the feast, Jesus stood and cried, saying, If any man thirst, let him come unto me, and drink.

> He that believeth on me, as the scripture hath said, out of his belly shall flow rivers of living water. (John 7:37-38)

Is not the Lord, the creator of the universe, able to fulfill His promises? He has promised life and life abundant! Surely we can believe Him! His faithfulness is unto all generations!

> Ho, every one that thirsteth, come ye to the waters, and he that hath no money; come ye, buy and eat; yea, come, buy wine and milk without money and without price.

> Wherefore do ye spend money for that which is not bread? and your labour for that which satisfieth not? hearken diligently unto me, and eat ye that which is good, and let your soul delight itself in fatness.

> Incline your ear, and come unto me: hear, and your soul shall live. . . .

> For my thoughts are not your thoughts, neither are your ways my ways, saith the Lord.

> For as the heavens are higher than the earth, so are my ways higher than your ways, and my thoughts than your thoughts. (Isa. 55:1-3, 8, 9)

HO, EVERY ONE THAT THIRSTETH, COME YE TO THE WATERS. . . .

NOTES

Part One: PSYCHOTHERAPY: HELP OR HARM?

1. Alvin Sanoff, "Psychiatry Runs into an Identity Crisis." *U. S. News and World Report*, Oct. 9 , 1978, p. 64.
2. Eliot Marshall, "The Profession of Psychiatry Is Getting a Bit Paranoid." *Los Angeles Herald Examiner*, Sept. 10, 1978, p. E-4.
3. Stephen J. Morse and Robert I. Watson, Jr. *Psychotherapies: A Comparative Casebook.* New York: Holt, Rinehart, and Winston, 1977, p. 9.
4. Perry London, "The Psychotherapy Boom." *Psychology Today*, June 1974, p. 63.
5. *Ibid.*, p. 68.
6. Franklin D. Chu and Sharland Trotter. *The Madness Establishment.* New York: Grossman Publishers, 1974, p. xxi.
7. *Ibid.*, p. 206.
8. Jerome D. Frank, "An Overview of Psychotherapy." *Overview of the Psychotherapies*, Gene Usdin, ed. New York: Brunner/Mazel, 1975, p. 7.
9. Sharland Trotter, "Nader Group Releases First Consumer Guide to Psychotherapists." *APA Monitor*, Dec. 1975, p. 11.
10. Frank, *op. cit.*, p. 8.
11. Leo Rosten, "Unhappiness Is Not a Disease," *Reader's Digest*, July 1978, p. 176.
12. Irving Schneider, "Images of the Mind: Psychiatry in the Commercial Film." *The American Journal of Psychiatry*, 134:6, June 1977, pp. 613-619.
13. Hans J. Eysenck, "The Effects of Psychotherapy: An Evaluation." *Journal of Consulting Psychology*, Vol. 16, 1952, p. 322.
14. *Ibid.*, pp. 322, 323.
15. Hans J. Eysenck, "New Ways in Psychotherapy." *Psychology Today*, June 1967, p. 40.
16. C. B. Truax and R. R. Carkhuff. *Toward Effective Counseling*

and Psychotherapy: Training and Practice. Chicago: Aldine, 1967, p. 5.

17. L. Luborsky, B. Singer, and L. Luborsky, "Comparative Studies of Psychotherapies." Archives of General Psychiatry. Vol. 32, 1975, pp. 995-1008.

18. Hans H. Strupp, Suzanne W. Hadley, Beverly Gomes-Schwartz. Psychotherapy for Better or Worse. New York: Jason Aronson, Inc., 1977, p. 340.

19. Ibid., pp. 115-116.

20. Suzanne W. Hadley, National Institute of Mental Health, personal letter, March 6, 1978, p. 5.

21. Richard B. Stuart. Trick or Treatment: How and When Psychotherapy Fails. Champaign: Research Press, 1970. p. i.

22. Ibid., p. 197.

23. Strupp, Hadley, and Gomes-Schwartz, op. cit., p. 51.

24. Ibid., p. 83.

25. Ibid.

26. Ernest Havemann, "Alternatives to Analysis." Playboy, Nov. 1969, p. 134.

27. Morris Parloff, "Shopping for the Right Therapy." Saturday Review, Feb. 21, 1976, p. 14.

28. Thomas Szasz. The Myth of Psychotherapy. Garden City: Anchor Press / Doubleday, 1978, p. xxiii.

29. Michael Scriven, quoted in "Psychotherapy Can Be Dangerous," by Allen Bergin, Psychology Today, Nov. 1975, p. 96.

30. O. Hobart Mowrer. The Crisis in Psychiatry and Religion. Princeton: D. Van Nostrand Co., Inc., 1961, p. 60.

Part Two: MIND/BODY . . . BODY/MIND

1. Frederick Evans, "The Power of a Sugar Pill." Psychology Today, April 1974, p. 59.

2. Ibid., p. 56.

3. Norman Cousins, "The Mysterious Placebo: How Mind Helps Medicine Work." Saturday Review, Oct. 1, 1977, p. 12.

4. Ching-piao Chien, "Drugs and Rehabilitation in Schizophrenia." Drugs in Combination with Other Therapies, Milton Greenblatt, ed. New York: Grune and Stratton, 1975, pp. 21-22.

5. Norman Cousins, "Anatomy of an Illness (as Perceived by the Patient)," Saturday Review, May 28, 1977, p. 48.

6. Meyer Friedman and Ray H. Rosenman, Type A Behavior and Your Heart. New York: Alfred A. Knopf, 1974, p. 53.

7. Ibid., p. 59.

8. Hans Selye. The Stress of Life. New York: McGraw-Hill, 1956. Stress without Distress. Philadelphia: J. B. Lippincott, 1974.

9. Kenneth R. Pelletier, "Mind as Healer, Mind as Slayer." Psy-

chology Today, Feb. 1977, p. 35.

10. *Ibid.*, p. 36.

11. James Hassett, "Teaching Yourself to Relax." *Psychology Today*, Aug. 1978, p. 28.

12. Cousins, "The Mysterious Placebo," *op. cit.*, p. 11.

13. Barbara Fish. "Research Today or Tragedy Tomorrow," *American Journal of Psychiatry*, Vol. 128, No. 2, May 1972, p. 1439.

14. Seymour Kety, "Mental Illness in the Biological and Adoptive Families of Adopted Schizophrenics." *American Journal of Psychiatry*, Vol. 128, No. 3, Sept. 1971, p. 306.

15. Irving I. Gottesman and James Shields. *Schizophrenia and Genetics: A Twin Study Vantage Point.* New York: Academic Press, 1972, p. 316.

16. *Ibid.*, p. 316.

17. Leonard L. Heston, "The Genetics of Schizophrenic and Schizoid Disease." *Science*, Jan. 1970, p. 255.

18. Remi J. Cadoret, "Evidence for Genetic Inheritance of Primary Affective Disorder in Adoptees." *American Journal of Psychiatry*, Vol. 135, No. 4, April 1978, p. 463.

19. Gary Miner, "The Evidence for Genetic Components in the Neuroses." *Archives of General Psychiatry*, Vol. 29, July 1973, p. 117.

20. A. A. Kawi and B. Pasamanick, "Prenatal and Paranatal Factors in the Development of Childhood Reading Disorders." *Monographs of the Society for Research in Child Development*, Vol. 24, No. 4, 1959, p. 61.

21. Seymour Kety, "It's Not All in Your Head." *Saturday Review*, Feb. 21, 1976, p. 29.

22. *Ibid.*, p. 28,

23. Philip R. A. May. *Treatment of Schizophrenia.* New York: Science House, 1968, pp. 231-237.

24. *Ibid.*, p. 232.

25. Frank J. Ayd, Jr., "Psychotropic Drug Combinations: Good and Bad." *Drugs in Combination with Other Therapies*, Milton Greenblatt, ed. New York: Grune and Stratton, 1975, p. 165.

26. Thomas Szasz, "Nobody Should Decide Who Goes to the Mental Hospital." *The Co-Evolution Quarterly*, Summer 1978, p. 59.

27. Elliot S. Valenstein, "Science-Fiction Fantasy and the Brain." *Psychology Today*, July 1978, p. 31.

28. *Ibid.*, p. 38.

29. Ben F. Feingold. *Why Your Child Is Hyperactive.* New York: Random House, 1975.

30. K. E. Moyer, "The Physiology of Violence: Allergy and Aggression." *Psychology Today*, July 1975, p. 77.

31. Allan Cott, "Orthomolecular Treatment: A Biochemical Approach to Treatment of Schizophrenia." New York: American

Schizophrenia Association, p. 4.

32. E. Fuller Torrey, "Tracking the Causes of Madness." *Psychology Today*, March 1979, p. 91.

33. E. Fuller Torrey, "Schizophrenia: Sense and Nonsense." *Psychology Today*, Nov. 1977, p. 157.

34. Julian Meltzoff and Melvin Kornreich. *Research in Psychotherapy*. New York: Atherton Press, Inc., 1970, p. 64.

35. Torrey, "Tracking the Causes of Madness," *op. cit.*, p. 79.

36. Torrey, "Schizophrenia: Sense and Nonsense," *op. cit.*, p. 157.

37. Normal Cousins, "The Victims Are Not Just the Ill." *Saturday Review*, Feb. 21, 1976, p. 5.

38. Sydney Walker III, "Blood Sugar and Emotional Storms: Sugar Doctors Push Hypoglycemia." *Psychology Today*, July 1975, p. 74.

39. Allen Bergin, "Psychotherapy Can Be Dangerous." *Psychology Today*, Nov. 1975, p. 96.

40. I. S. Cooper. *The Victim Is Always the Same*. New York: Harper and Row, 1973.

41. Ronald P. Lesser and Stanley Fahn, "Dystonia: A Disorder Often Misdiagnosed as a Conversion Reaction." *American Journal of Psychiatry*, Vol. 135, No. 3, March 1978, p. 350.

42. Michael Chase, "The Matriculating Brain." *Psychology Today*, June 1973, p. 82.

Part Three: PSYCHOTHERAPY: QUESTIONS, CRITIQUES, CRITICISMS

1. Sigmund Koch, ed. *Psychology: A Study of a Science*. New York: McGraw-Hill, 1959-63.

2. Sigmund Koch, "Psychology Cannot Be a Coherent Science." *Psychology Today*, Sept. 1969, p. 66.

3. *Ibid.*, p. 67.

4. *Ibid.*, p. 67.

5. Sigmund Koch, "The Image of Man in Encounter Groups." *The American Scholar*, Vol. 42, No. 4, Autumn 1973, p. 636.

6. Gordon Allport. *Pattern and Growth in Personality*. New York: Holt, Rinehart & Winston, Inc., 1961, p. 10.

7. *Ibid.*, pp. 8, 9.

8. Hillel J. Einhorn and Robin M. Hogarth, "Confidence in Judgment: Persistence of the Illusion of Validity." *Psychological Review*, Vol. 85, No. 5, 1978, p. 395.

9. Arthur Janov. *The Primal Scream*. New York: Dell Publishing Co., Inc., 1970, p. 19.

10. Bertrand Russell. *The Impact of Science on Society*. New York: Simon and Schuster, 1953, p. 18.

11. Carlo L. Lastrucci. *The Scientific Approach: Basic Principles of*

the Scientific Method. Cambridge: Schenkman Publishing Co., Inc., 1967, p. 115.

12. Karl Popper, "Scientific Theory and Falsifiability." *Perspectives in Philosophy*, Robert N. Beck, ed. New York: Holt, Rinehart, Winston, 1975, p. 342.

13. *Ibid.*, p. 343.

14. *Ibid.*, p. 344.

15. *Ibid.*, p. 345.

16. *Ibid.*, p. 343.

17. *Ibid.*, p. 346.

18. Jerome Frank, "Therapeutic Factors in Psychotherapy." *American Journal of Psychotherapy*, Vol. 25, 1971, p. 356.

19. E. Fuller Torrey. *The Mind Game.* New York: Emerson Hall Publishers, Inc., 1972, p. 8.

20. Robert Rosenthal. *Experimental Effects in Behavioral Research.* New York: Appleton-Century-Crofts, 1966, p. vii.

21. Koch, "Psychology Cannot Be a Coherent Science," *op. cit.*, p. 66.

22. Frank, *op. cit.*, p. 356.

23. Jerome Frank, "An Overview of Psychotherapy." *Overview of the Psychotherapies*, Gene Usdin, ed. New York: Brunner/Mazel, 1975, p. 19.

24. Karl Menninger, quoted in *Science Digest*, July 1973, p. 14.

25. Thomas Szasz. *The Myth of Psychotherapy.* Garden City: Doubleday/Anchor Press, 1978, pp. 182-183.

26. Franklin D. Chu and Sharland Trotter. *The Madness Establishment.* New York: Grossman Publishers, 1974, p. 4.

27. Szasz, *op. cit.*, p. 7.

28. Thomas Szasz. *The Myth of Mental Illness.* New York: Harper and Row, 1974, p. 262.

29. E. Fuller Torrey. *The Death of Psychiatry.* Radnor: Chilton Book Company, 1974, p. 24.

30. J. Benedict, "Battle Royal Over Inkblot Tests." *Science Digest*, Oct. 1971, pp. 48, 53.

31. Richard B. Stuart. *Trick or Treatment: How and When Psychotherapy Fails.* Champaign: Research Press, 1970. p. 86.

32. K. B. Little, "Problems in the Validation of Projective Techniques." *Journal of Projective Techniques*, Vol. 23, 1959, p. 287.

33. Thomas Szasz. *The Manufacture of Madness.* New York: Harper & Row, Publishers, 1970, p. 35.

34. Leslie Phillips and Joseph Smith. *Rorschach Interpretation: Advanced Technique.* New York: Grune and Stratton, 1953, p. 149.

35. Arthur Jensen. *The Sixth Mental Measurements Yearbook.* Oscar Krisen Buros, ed. Highland Park: The Gryphon Press, 1965, p. 501.

36. Charles C. McArthur. *The Seventh Mental Measurements Year-*

book, Oscar Krisen Buros, ed. Highland Park: The Gryphon Press, 1972, p. 443.

37. Jensen, *op. cit.*, p. 501.
38. Hans H. Strupp, Suzanne W. Hadley, Beverly Gomes-Schwartz. *Psychotherapy for Better or Worse.* New York: Jason Aronson, Inc., 1977, p. 115.
39. Stuart, *op. cit.*, pp. 73-74.
40. *Ibid.*, p. 70.
41. *Ibid.*, pp. 71-72.
42. *Ibid.*, p. 72.
43. David L. Rosenhan, "On Being Sane in Insane Places." *Science,* Vol. 179, Jan. 1973, p. 252.
44. *Ibid.*, p. 252.
45. *Ibid.*, p. 253.
46. *Ibid.*, p. 252.
47. David Rosenhan, quoted in *Science Digest*, July 1973, p. 12.
48. Rosenhan, *op. cit.*, p. 252.
49. *Ibid.*, p. 252.
50. *Ibid.*, p. 257.
51. *Brain/Mind*, Nov. 6, 1978, p. 1.
52. Rosenhan, *op. cit.*, p. 257.
53. Abraham Halpern, quoted by James Gleick, "The Guilty by Insanity Plea Needs To Be Re-Examined." *Los Angeles Herald Examiner*, Sept. 10, 1978, p. E-4.
54. Jay Ziskin, quoted by James Gleick, *L. A. Herald Examiner*, Sept. 10, 1978, p. E-4.
55. Samuel Yochelson and Stanton Samenow. *The Criminal Personality.* New York: Aronson, Jason, Inc., Vol. 1, 1976; Vol. 2, 1977.
56. Samuel Yochelson and Stanton Samenow, quoted by Michael Serrill, "A Cold New Look at the Criminal Mind," *Psychology Today*, Feb. 1978, p. 89.
57. *Ibid.*, p. 89.
58. Strupp, Hadley, Gomes-Schwartz, *op. cit.*, p. 19.

Part Four: POLLUTED STREAMS

1. James C. Coleman and Constance L. Hammen. *Contemporary Psychology and Effective Behavior.* Glenview: Scott, Foresman and Company, 1974, p. 35.
2. Stephen J. Morse and Robert Watson, Jr. *Psychotherapies: A Comparative Casebook.* New York: Holt, Rinehart and Winston, 1977, p. 10.
3. Robert W. McCarley, "Where Dreams Come From: A New Theory." *Psychology Today*, December 1978, pp. 54-65, 141.
4. Sigmund Freud. *Three Essays on the Theory of Sexuality.* (1905) SE, Vol. vii. London: Hogarth Press, 1953, p. 226.

5. Thomas Szasz. *The Myth of Psychotherapy*. Garden City: Doubleday/Anchor Press, 1978, p. 133.
6. Alvin Sanoff, "Psychiatry Runs into an Identity Crisis," *U.S. News and World Report*, Oct. 9, 1978, p. 64.
7. O. Hobart Mowrer. *The Crisis in Psychiatry and Religion*. Princeton: D. Van Nostrand Co., Inc., 1961, p. 222.
8. *Ibid.*, p. 175.
9. E. Fuller Torrey. *The Death of Psychiatry*. Radnor: Chilton Book Company, 1974, p. 24.
10. Jim Swan, "Mater and Nannie . . . ." *American Imago*, Spring 1974, p. 10.
11. *Ibid.*, p. 10.
12. *Ibid.*, p. 10.
13. Edward C. Whitmont, "Jungian Analysis Today." *Psychology Today*, December 1972, p. 70.
14. Mowrer, *op. cit.*, p. 70.
15. Sigmund Freud. *The Ego and the Id*. Translated by Joan Riviere; revised and edited by James Strachey. New York: W. W. Norton and Company, Inc., 1960, p. 13.
16. Lewis Carroll. *Alice's Adventures in Wonderland*, 1865.
17. Jerome Kagan, "The Parental Love Trap." *Psychology Today*, Aug. 1978, p. 61.
18. Victor and Mildred Goertzel. *Cradles of Eminence*. Boston: Little, Brown and Company, 1962.
19. Samuel Yochelson and Stanton Samenow. *The Criminal Personality*. New York: Jason Aronson, Inc., Vol. 1, 1976; Vol. 2, 1977.
20. Simon Dinitz, quoted in "The Criminal Personality in Perspective," Michael Serrill. *Psychology Today*, February 1978, p. 92.
21. Szasz, *op. cit.*, p. 167.
22. William Glasser, tape of first class of the Pastoral Counseling Institute at the Institute for Reality Therapy, November 7, 1969.
23. Sigmund Freud, "Formations Regarding the Two Principles of Mental Functioning," quoted in *Reality Therapy*, William Glasser. New York: Harper and Row, 1965. p. xix.
24. Sigmund Freud, "Sexuality in the Aetiology of the Neuroses" (1898), *Collected Papers*, Vol. 1. New York: Basic Books, Inc., 1959, p. 220.
25. Sigmund Freud. *The Origins of Psychoanalysis: Letters, Drafts and Notes to Wilhelm Fliess* (1887-1902). Garden City: Anchor Books, 1957, p. 67.
26. Benjamin Spock. *Baby and Child Care*. New York: Pocket Books, Inc., 1957.
27. Benjamin Spock, "How Not to Bring up a Bratty Child." *Redbook*, Feb. 1974, p. 31.

28. *Ibid.*, p. 31.
29. *Ibid.*, p. 29.
30. *Ibid.*, p. 31.
31. Mowrer, *op. cit.*, p. 123.
32. O. Hobart Mowrer. *Morality and Mental Health.* Chicago: Rand McNally & Company, 1967, p. 17.
33. *Ibid.*, p. 17.
34. Szasz, *op. cit.*, p. 45.
35. Jay Haley. *Strategies of Psychotherapy.* New York: Grune & Stratton, Inc., 1963, p. 82.
36. Eileen Keerdoja, "The 'Screaming Cure,' " *Newsweek*, July 10, 1978, p. 12.
37. Arthur Janov. *The Primal Scream.* New York: Dell Publishing Co., Inc., 1970.
38. Keerdoja, *op. cit.*, p. 12.
39. Janov, *op. cit.*, pp. 28-29.
40. *Ibid.*, p. 20.
41. *Ibid.*, p. 154.
42. *Ibid.*, p. 134.
43. Daniel Casriel. *A Scream Away From Happiness.* New York: Grosset and Dunlap, Inc., 1972.
44. Martin Gross. *The Psychological Society.* New York: Random House, 1978, p. 283.
45. Leonard Berkowitz, "The Case for Bottling Up Rage." *Psychology Today*, July 1973, p. 28.
46. *Ibid.*, p. 31.
47. *Ibid.*, p. 31.
48. *Ibid.*, p. 26.
49. Arthur Burton, ed. *Encounter.* San Francisco: Jossey-Bass, Inc., 1969, p. 12.
50. *Ibid.*, p. 24.
51. Abraham Maslow, quoted by Sigmund Koch in "Psychology Cannot Be a Coherent Science." *Psychology Today*, Sept. 1969, p. 68.
52. Casriel, *op. cit.*, p. 8.
53. Carl Rogers. *Carl Rogers on Encounter Groups.* New York: Harper and Row, 1970, p. 167.
54. *Ibid.*, p. vi.
55. Morton A. Lieberman, Irvin Yalom, and Matthew Miles. *Encounter Groups: First Facts.* New York: Basic Books, Inc., 1973, p. 74.
56. *Ibid.*, p. 11.
57. *Ibid.*, p. 95.
58. Morton A. Lieberman, Irvin Yalom, and Matthew Miles, "Encounter: The Leader Makes the Difference." *Psychology Today*, March 1973, p. 74.

59. *Ibid.*, p. 74.
60. Jerome Frank, "An Overview of Psychotherapy." *Overview of the Psychotherapies*, Gene Usdin, ed. New York: Brunner/ Mazel, 1975, p. 9.
61. Lieberman, Yalom, Miles, *op. cit.*, p. 74.
62. Rodney Luther, quoted by Kurt Back, "The Group Can Comfort But It Can't Cure." *Psychology Today*, December 1972, p. 32.
63. Frederick Perls. *Gestalt Therapy Verbatim*. Lafayette: Real People Press, 1969, p. 75.
64. Sigmund Koch, "The Image of Man in Encounter Groups." *The American Scholar*, Vol. 42, No. 4, Autumn 1973, p. 639.
65. Burton, *op. cit.*, p. x.
66. R.C. Devon Heck and Jennifer L. Thompson, "Est: Salvation or Swindle?" *San Francisco Magazine*, January 1976, p. 22.
67. Adelaide Bry. *Est: 60 Hours that Transform Your Life*. New York: Harper and Row, 1976, p. 31.
68. *Ibid.*, p. 31.
69. *Newsweek*, Kenneth Woodward, "Super-Salesman of est." Sept. 6, 1976, p. 59.
70. Mark Brewer, " 'We're Gonna Tear You Down and Put You Back Together.' " *Psychology Today*, August 1975, p. 35.
71. *Ibid.*, p. 39.
72. *Ibid.*, p. 39.
73. *Ibid.*, p. 88.
74. Bry, *op. cit.*, p. 56.
75. *Ibid.*, p. 148.
76. *Ibid.*, p. 1.
77. Woodward, *op. cit.*, p. 59.
78. Bry, *op. cit.*, p. 48.
79. *Ibid.*, p. 30.
80. *Ibid.*, p. 156.
81. *Ibid.*, p. 74.
82. *Ibid.*, p. 96.
83. *Ibid.*, pp. 28-30.
84. *Ibid.*, p. 35.
85. *Ibid.*, p. 153.
86. " 'Transformation of a Man': What Makes Erhard Run?" *Los Angeles Times*, Book Section, November 5, 1978, p. 14.
87. Peter Marin, "The New Narcissism." *Harper's*, Oct. 1975, p. 45.
88. *Ibid.*, p. 48.
89. Charles Tart, ed. *Transpersonal Psychologies*. New York: Harper and Row, Publishers, 1975.
90. Daniel Goleman, "The Reception of Eastern Psychologies in the West." The Center for the Study of Democratic Institutions Dialogue Discussion Paper, Monday, June 5, 1978, p. 2.

214

91. Jacob Needleman, "Psychiatry and the Sacred." *On the Way to Self Knowledge*, edited by Jacob Needleman and Dennis Lewis. New York: Alfred A. Knopf, 1976, p. 7.
92. *Arica 1978*. New York: Arica Institute, Inc., p. 14.
93. Sam Keen, " 'We Have No Desire to Strengthen the Ego or Make It Happy.' " *Psychology Today*, July 1973, pp. 64-72.
94. Colin Campbell, "Transcendence Is as American as Ralph Waldo Emerson." *Psychology Today*, April 1974, p. 37.
95. *Brain/Mind Bulletin*, Aug. 7, 1978, p. 1.
96. Harold Bloomfield, Michael Cain, and Dennis Jaffe. *TM Discovering Inner Energy and Overcoming Stress*. New York: Delacorte Press, 1975, p. 11.
97. *Ibid.*, p. 10.
98. *Ibid.*, p. 11.
99. Richard D. Scott. *Transcendental Misconceptions*. San Diego: Beta Books, 1978.
100. Robert Ornstein, "The Container Vs. the Content." *Psychology Today*, Sept. 1976, p. 39.
101. Gary Schwartz, " 'TM Relaxes Some People and Makes Them Feel Better.' " *Psychology Today*, April 1974, p. 39.
102. Denise Denniston and Peter McWilliams. *The TM Book*. Allen Park: Three Rivers Press, 1975, pp. 90-99.
103. Ornstein, *op. cit.*, p. 39.
104. Leon Otis, "If Well-Integrated but Anxious Try TM." *Psychology Today*, April 1974, p. 46.
105. Schwartz, *op. cit.*, p. 44.
106. *Ibid.*, p. 43.
107. *Brain/Mind*, Feb. 5, 1979, p. 1.
108. Otis, *op. cit.*, p. 46.
109. Schwartz, *op. cit.*, p. 44.
110. Dan Goleman, "Transcendental Meditation Goes Public." *Psychology Today*, Nov. 1975, p. 90.
111. Schwartz, *op. cit.*, p. 44.
112. Maharishi Mahesh Yogi. *Meditations of Maharishi Mahesh Yogi*. New York: Bantam Books, 1968, p. 119.
113. John Wren-Lewis, "Supermarket Pseudoscience or a New Transcendentalism?" *Psychology Today*, April 1976, p. 66.
114. Theodore Roszak. *Unfinished Animal: The Acquarian Frontier and the Evolution of Consciousness*. New York: Harper and Row, 1975.
115. Sam Keen, "Oscar Ichazo and the Arica Institute." *Psychology Today*, July 1973, p. 66.
116. Ornstein, *op. cit.*, p. 36.
117. Kenneth Woodward, "Getting Your Head Together." *Newsweek*, Sept. 6, 1976, p. 57.
118. Ornstein, *op. cit.*, p. 36.

Part Five: ANGELS OF LIGHT

1. *Newsweek*, Sept. 6, 1976, p. 57.
2. Jay Haley. *Strategies of Psychotherapy*. New York: Grune & Stratton, Inc., 1963, p. 71.
3. *Ibid.*, p. 82.
4. Calvin S. Hall and Gardner Lindzey. *Theories of Personality*. New York: John Wiley & Sons, 1957, p. 476.
5. Carl Rogers. *On Becoming a Person*. Boston: Houghton Mifflin, 1961, p. 8.
6. *Ibid.*, p. 8.
7. *Ibid.*, p. 8.
8. *Ibid.*, p. 8.
9. Carl Rogers, "Some Personal Learnings about Interpersonal Relationships," 33 min. 16mm film developed by Dr. Charles K. Ferguson. University of California Extension Media Center, Berkeley, Calif., film #6785.
10. Carl Rogers in *Psychology: A Study of a Science*, Vol. 3, Sigmund Koch, ed. New York: McGraw-Hill, 1959, p. 209.
11. Hillel J. Einhorn and Robin M. Hogarth, "Confidence in Judgment: Persistence of the Illusion of Validity." *Psychological Review*, Vol. 85, No. 5, 1978, p. 414.
12. Paul C. Vitz. *Psychology as Religion: The Cult of Self Worship*. Grand Rapids: William B. Eerdmans Publishing Company, 1977.
13. William Glasser. *Reality Therapy*. New York: Harper and Row, 1965, p. 44.
14. *Ibid.*, p. 53.
15. *Ibid.*, p. 6.
16. *Ibid.*, p. 6.
17. *Ibid.*, p. 13.
18. *Ibid.*, pp. 10-11.
19. *Ibid.*, p. 12.
20. *Ibid.*, p. 9.
21. *Ibid.*, p. 57.
22. Thomas Harris. *I'M OK—YOU'RE OK: A Practical Guide to Transactional Analysis*. New York: Harper and Row, 1967, p. 26.
23. *Ibid.*, p. 27.
24. *Ibid.*, p. 41.
25. *Ibid.*, pp. 43, 37.
26. *Ibid.*, p. 50.
27. *Ibid.*, p. 52.
28. *Ibid.*, p. 5.
29. *Ibid.*, p. 39.
30. *Ibid.*, p. 243.
31. *Ibid.*, p. 28.

32. *Ibid.*, p. 42.
33. *Ibid.*, p. 225-226.
34. *Ibid.*, p. 239.
35. *Ibid.*, p. 184.
36. *Ibid.*, p. 230.
37. *Ibid.*, p. 241.
38. *Ibid.*, p. 227.
39. *Ibid.*, p. 227.
40. *Ibid.*, p. 228.
41. *Ibid.*, pp. 230-231.

Part Six: THE PSYCHOLOGICAL WAY / THE SPIRITUAL WAY

1. Charles Tart. *Transpersonal Psychologies.* New York: Harper and Row, Publishers, 1975, p. 5.
2. Paavo Airola, "Optimum Nutrition: Foundation for Holistic Health." Lecture at Santa Barbara City College, Oct. 11, 1977.
3. Paul Brenner, "Health Is a Question of Balance." Lecture at Santa Barbara City College, April 18, 1978.
4. Peter Koestenbaum. *The New Image of the Person.* Westport: Greenwood Press, 1978.
5. Hans Strupp and Suzanne Hadley, "Specific Versus Nonspecific Factors in Psychotherapy: A Controlled Study of Outcome," unpublished paper on Vanderbilt Study, 1977, pp. 1, 2.
6. Allen Bergin and Michael Lambert, "The Evaluation of Therapeutic Outcomes." *Handbook of Psychotherapy and Behavior Change: An Empirical Analysis*, 2nd Ed. Sol Garfield and Allen Bergin, eds. New York: John Wiley and Sons, 1978, p. 180.
7. Jerome Frank. *Persuasion and Healing.* New York: Schocken Books, 1961, 1974 ed., p. 325.
8. Thomas Szasz. *The Myth of Psychotherapy.* Garden City: Doubleday/Anchor Press, 1978, p. 35.
9. Arthur K. Shapiro interview. *The Psychological Society* by Martin Gross. New York: Random House, 1978, p. 230.
10. Frank, *op. cit.*, p. 329.
11. Jerome Frank. *Persuasion and Healing.* Baltimore: Johns Hopkins Press, 1961, p. 72.
12. "Guilt Feeling Gone? Could Be 'In the Bag' " (AP) *Santa Barbara News Press*, February 26, 1978, p. A-1.
13. Frank, *op. cit.*, 1961 edition, p. 60.
14. Thomas Kiernan. *Shrinks, Etc.* New York: Dial Press, 1974, p. 255.
15. Paul Halmos. *The Faith of the Counselors.* New York: Schocken Books, 1966, 1970 ed., Social Service Review comment on back cover.

16. *Ibid.*, p. 51.
17. Szasz, *op. cit.*, p. 35.
18. Jay Haley. *Strategies of Psychotherapy*. New York: Grune & Stratton, Inc., 1963, pp. 183-184.
19. Alvin Sanoff, "Psychatry Runs Into an Identity Crisis," *U.S. News and World Report*, Oct. 9, 1978, p. 63.
20. Millard J. Sall. *Faith, Psychology and Christian Maturity*. Grand Rapids: Zondervan Publishing House, 1975, 1977 ed., p. 13.
21. Ruth G. Matarazzo, "Research on the Teaching and Learning of Psychotherapeutic Skills." *Handbook of Psychotherapy and Behavior Change: An Empirical Analysis*. Allen Bergin and Sol Garfield, eds. New York: Wiley, 1971, p. 910.
22. Frank, *op. cit.*, 1974 edition, p. 167.
23. Strupp and Hadley, *op. cit.*, p. 5.
24. *Ibid.*, p. 17.
25. E. Fuller Torrey. *The Death of Psychiatry*. Radnor: Chilton Book Company, 1974, p. 58.
26. Hans Strupp, "On the Basic Ingredients of Psychotherapy." *Journal of Consulting and Clinical Psychology*, Vol. 41, 1973, pp. 1-8.
27. Haley, *op. cit.*, p. 69.
28. E. Fuller Torrey, "The Case for the Indigenous Therapist." *Archives of General Psychiatry*, Vol. 20, March 1969, p. 367.
29. Frank, *op. cit.*, 1974 edition, p. 161.
30. Matarazzo, *op. cit.*, p. 911.
31. *Ibid.*, p. 915.
32. Torrey, "The Case for the Indigenous Therapist," *op. cit.*, p. 365.
33. Hans Strupp, Suzanne Hadley, and Beverly Gomes-Schwartz. *Psychotherapy for Better or Worse*. New York: Jason Aronson, Inc., 1977, p. 66.
34. Szasz, *op. cit.*, inside jacket cover.
35. Hans Strupp, "Psychoanalysis, 'Focal Psychotherapy,' and the Nature of Therapeutic Influence." *Archives of General Psychiatry*, January 1975, p. 133.
36. Frances J. Roberts. *On the Highroad of Surrender*. Ojai: The King's Press, 1973, p. 54.
37. Thomas Szasz. *The Myth of Mental Illness*. New York: Harper and Row, 1974, p. 263.
38. Karl Menninger. *Whatever Became of Sin?* New York: Hawthorn Books, Inc., 1973, p. 18.
39. Henry Fairlie. *The Seven Deadly Sins Today*. Washington: New Republic Books, 1978, jacket cover.
40. Donald T. Campbell, "On the Conflicts Between Biological and Social Evolution and Between Psychology and Moral Tradition." *American Psychologist*, December 1975, p. 1103.

41. *Ibid.*, p. 1104.
42. *Ibid.*, p. 1120.
43. *Ibid.*, p. 1120.
44. *APA Monitor.* December 1975, p. 4.
45. Szasz. *The Myth of Psychotherapy, op. cit.*, p. xvii.
46. Stephen J. Morse and Robert Watson, Jr., *Psychotherapies: A Comparative Casebook.* New York: Holt, Rinehart and Winston, 1977, p. 3.

Part Seven: BROKEN CISTERNS AND LIVING WATERS

1. Morris Parloff, "Shopping for the Right Therapy." *Saturday Review*, Feb. 21, 1976, p. 14.
2. Sigmund Freud. *The Future of an Illusion.* Translated and edited by James Strachey. New York: W. W. Norton and Company, Inc., 1961, p. 43.
3. Thomas Szasz. *The Myth of Psychotherapy.* Garden City: Doubleday/Anchor Press, 1978, p. 173.
4. George E. Atwood and Silvan S. Tomkins, "On the Subjectivity of Personality Theory." *Journal of the History of the Behavioral Sciences*, 12 (1976), p. 167.
5. Szasz, *op. cit.*, p. 139.
6. *Ibid.*, p. 146.
7. *Ibid.*, p. 140.
8. C. G. Jung. *Memories, Dreams, Reflections*, ed. by Aniela Jaffe, trans. by Richard and Clara Winston. New York: Pantheon, 1963, p. 55.
9. Viktor Von Weizsaecker, "Reminiscences of Freud and Jung." *Freud and the Twentieth Century*, B. Nelson, ed. New York: Meridian, 1957, p. 72.
10. Jacob Needleman. *A Sense of the Cosmos.* Garden City: Doubleday and Co., Inc., 1975, p. 107.
11. Arthur Burton, ed. *Encounter.* San Francisco: Jossey-Bass Inc., 1969, p. 11.
12. Szasz, *op. cit.*, p. 188.
13. *Ibid.*, pp. 104-105.
14. *Ibid.*, pp. 27-28.
15. *Ibid.*, p. 188.
16. Herbert Lazarus. *How to Get Your Money's Worth out of Psychiatry.* Los Angeles: Sherbourne Press, Inc., 1973, p. 229.
17. Szasz, *op. cit.*, p. 32.
18. Julian Meltzoff and Melvin Kornreich. *Research in Psychotherapy.* New York: Atherton Press, Inc. 1970, p. 465.
19. John T. McNeill. *A History of the Cure of Souls.* New York: Harper and Row, 1951, p. vii.

20. *Ibid.*, p. 167.
21. *Ibid.*, p. 168.
22. Elaine Warren, "Sex in Therapy," three part series. *Los Angeles Herald Examiner.* Nov. 26, 1978, pp. A-1, 12; Nov. 27, 1978, pp. A-1, C-4; Nov. 28, 1978, pp. A-1, C-6. Dan Rather and Steve Glauber, "Fifty Minutes," transcript of *60 Minutes*, Vol. x, No. 25, CBS-TV, Feb. 19, 1978.
23. Szasz. *The Myth of Psychotherapy, op. cit.*, p. xviii.
24. *Ibid.*, p. xxiv.
25. *Ibid.*, p. 26.
26. Thomas Szasz, "Nobody Should Decide Who Goes to the Mental Hospital." *Co-Evolution Quarterly*, Summer 1978, p. 60.
27. Jerome Frank, "Therapeutic Factors in Psychotherapy." *American Journal of Psychotherapy*, Vol. 25, 1971, p. 360.
28. Paul D. Morris. *Love Therapy*. Wheaton: Tyndale, 1974, p. 32.
29. O. Quentin Hyder. *The Christian's Handbook of Psychiatry*. Old Tappan: Fleming H. Revell Co., 1971.
30. Tim LaHaye. *Spirit-Controlled Temperament*. Wheaton: Tyndale, 1966.
31. Christopher Lasch. *The Culture of Narcissism*. New York: W. W. Norton and Company, Inc., 1978, inside jacket cover.
32. Morris Netherton and Nancy Shiffrin. *Past Lives Therapy*. New York: William Morrow and Co., 1978.
33. Needleman, *op. cit.*, p. 109.
34. Ralph Metzner. *Maps of Consciousness*. New York: Macmillan Co., 1971.
35. Walter Bromberg. *From Shaman to Psychotherapist*. Chicago: Henry Regnery Company, 1975, p. 336.
36. Paul Billheimer. *Don't Waste Your Sorrows*. Fort Washington: Christian Literature Crusade, 1977, p. 89.
37. Lawrence J. Crabb, Jr., "Moving the Couch into the Church," *Christianity Today*, Sept. 22, 1978, p. 18.
38. Ray Stedman. *Folk Psalms of Faith*. Glendale: Regal Books, 1973, p. 41.

INDEX

acceptance of person, in spiritual counseling, 169-70

Adler, Alfred, 47, 48

Allport, Gordon, 45, 66

American Psychological Association, 44

anxiety, 32, 34

Arica, 104-108

behaviorist model of psychotherapy, 66

Bible:
  as basis of spiritual counseling, 161, 166, 172, 173, 176, 197
  as basis of mental-emotional health, 11, 195-6, 197

biblical counseling, *see* spiritual counseling

biblical principles:
  as criterion to evaluate psychotherapies, 146-7
  and client-centered therapy, 120-24
  and Freud's morality, 82-3
  and Freud's psychic determinism, 78-80
  and Reality Therapy, 128-32
  and Transactional Analysis, 135-41

and psychotherapeutic principles, 25

biological origins of mental-emotional disorders, 31-8

body-mind relationship, 27-42

brain, 41, 52

Burton, Arthur, 92, 93, 97, 182

causes of mental-emotional disorders, 27-42

children:
  discipline, 83
  sexuality, *see* infantile sexuality

cholesterol and behavior, 29-30

church and psychotherapy, 184-204

client-centered therapy, 118-24

clinical judgment, 57

confession, 140, 169-70, 185, 186
  see also forgiveness; repentance; sin

criminal insanity, 61-2

cure of minds, 187, 189, 190, 191, 198, 202

cure of souls, 184-90, 192, 193, 202, 203

demonism, 187-8

depression, 34, 35

diagnosis of mental-emotional disorders, 38-41, 53-62
  interview, 57-8
  tests, 53-6